D0787282

COPING
W I T H

An Immigrant

Parent

Moira Davison Reynolds

THE ROSEN PUBLISHING GROUP, INC./NEW YORK

To Ron, Diana, Brittany, and Andrew

ABOUT THE AUTHOR ◇

A native of Northern Ireland, Moira Davison Reynolds was educated in the United States and Canada. She has a B.A. degree from Dalhousie University in Halifax, Nova Scotia, and a Ph.D. in biochemistry from Boston University.

Beginning her career in the hospital medical laboratory, she later was engaged in cancer research and taught biochemistry to medical students.

She is now a free-lance writer with several books to her credit. She has contributed to magazines and newspapers and often teaches an adult education course in writing nonfiction for publication.

Mrs. Reynolds has traveled extensively in both the United States and Canada. A supporter of various causes, she is a longtime member of Zonta International, a service organization of executive and professional women, and she is an enthusiastic volunteer for UNICEF. In 1979, Northern Michigan University honored her with a President's Award for Distinguished Citizenship.

She lives in Marquette, Michigan, with her husband. They are the parents of a son and the grandparents of a girl and a boy.

Contents

AUTHOR'S NOTE ◇

I am not an immigrant in the usual sense. I was born abroad but acquired American citizenship by birth because I was the child of American citizens. English is my native tongue.

My memory of much that happened during my pre-school years is dim, but one event stands out. When I was almost five, my mother brought me and my brother and sister to the United States to rejoin our father. As the ship approached New York on a foggy morning, I saw the Statue of Liberty. That sight I shall never forget. I know I could not have appreciated its meaning, but I am sure I sensed the excitement of others around us. I think that was the moment I became interested in immigrants. Later I spent several of my adolescent years in Canada, a country for which I have a high regard.

I wish to thank friends and acquaintances, too many to mention, who directed me to sources of help with this project. The resources of the Peter White Public Library in Marquette and of Northern Michigan University's Lydia Olson Library have been invaluable. I am especially indebted to Joanne Whitley of Superiorland Library Cooperative; she continues to locate whatever I need.

Moira Davison Reynolds
Marquette, Michigan

CHAPTER 1

Two Generations—
Two Cultures

[My daughter] calls us greenhorns and is ashamed of us.
—From an immigrant mother to
The Jewish Daily Forward, 1919.

"The Chinese food was wonderful when it was family," best-seller novelist Amy Tan once recalled, "but when my friends came over I was embarrassed."

Maria Aguirre, an immigrant* from Mexico who became a pediatrician, expressed similar feelings: When she found a tortilla in her lunch she fervently wished for Wonder Bread, "just to be normal."

Such feeling is common in first-generation Americans and Canadians. At best, adolescence is a difficult time. Additional problems are likely to surface when the younger generation attempts to become absorbed into a

---

*An immigrant moves into a country; an emigrant exits a country.

new culture while the parents insist on clinging to their old ways.

First names are likely candidates to cause embarrassment at school and on other occasions outside the home. Foreign names are sometimes Anglicized, which often disappoints parents and other relatives. Here are some actual cases: Jorge from El Salvador adopted the name George; Joo from Korea chose Jennifer; Phede from Haiti renamed himself Fred; Tien used his Vietnamese name when he was with his family, but at other times he substituted Tim. Betushka from Russia changed her name to Betty.

The language barrier is real. It is well expressed by William Kurelek in *They Sought a New World*: ". . . A few days later began the most traumatic experience of my pre-adult life—starting school. . . . The reason was language embarrassment. We would immediately start chattering in Ukrainian only to discover there was a kind of unwritten taboo on any language but English in a public school. . . . The teacher was staring at me. Then it hit me! I'd used the wrong language. I clammed up immediately and wished with all my heart that it was possible to sink beneath the floor." Kurelek, by the way, became a distinguished Canadian artist.

But English has to be mastered. It is needed for practical purposes such as following directions and filling in application forms; it is necessary to progress in school and careers. Even understanding jokes in English is frustrating for someone who is not versed in the language. Learning English becomes more difficult if another language is always spoken at home, as is usually the case with recent immigrants. But most children of immigrants want to learn English as quickly as possible and to speak it without an accent.

A special problem exists in Canada because it is a bilingual country. In some provinces it is clearly an advantage and occasionally a necessity to understand both English and French. However, trying to accomplish this imposes a double burden on a newcomer.

Teenagers from immigrant families tend to prefer the food their new friends eat to what their families have at home. In many cases, however, the mother continues to serve the same dishes she has been giving her children for years.

Money is usually scarce in the immigrant family. Often the children, at a young age, are expected to work without pay at various family enterprises. This may not be unreasonable, but having little or no leisure time, the young people find it difficult to make new friends, develop athletic skills, or pursue their own special interests.

The money issue is very important. As one high school teacher has noted, the first generation of American-born children want designer jeans, bicycles, digital watches, and more. When there is no money to pay for such things, their frustration increases.

Moral issues cause much argument. A sociology professor has said, "Many American values and customs which are very much part of the American way of life are seen [by Asian Indians] as evil. The American attitude toward sex . . . is viewed as immoral." So it is not surprising that dating among high schoolers is often forbidden. Another cause of contention is the expectation that children live at home until they marry. Foreign parents are still known to "arrange" marriages for their daughters. Although this is rather rare, it is bound to cause painful disagreements.

Very likely you have had firsthand experience with

such problems or know of similar cases. Constantin Galskoy, who became editor-in-chief of the Russian-language edition of *Reader's Digest*, relates his feelings soon after he arrived in the United States. He was then eleven and a Russian emigrant from Morocco: "I began to hide every hint of our foreignness—never discussing our family's customs, culture or Russian Orthodox religion. I didn't want to draw attention to anything that made me seem different."

If your parents have poor command of English, you may be embarrassed about it. You may even find yourself hoping that your classmates and friends never meet them. Perhaps another embarrassment is the type of clothes you are expected to wear. Somehow they never look quite right, no matter how much trouble your mother took with them.

You may be constantly pressed into chores that involve translating, letter-writing—whatever. And all because your parents can't speak or read English. You resent this. What is more important, you resent your parents' unyielding control as well as their overprotectiveness.

And you feel ashamed. These people who embarrass you and whom you resent are your mother and father. They love you. You are part of why they have sacrificed to come to another land. They want for you education and opportunities that never were and never will be open to them. So deep down, you feel guilt.

By selecting this book to read, you have shown a desire to do something about the situation. An important step toward solving a problem is to recognize it. You have already done that. And by so doing, you have shown maturity.

Progress cannot come without understanding. In the pages ahead we'll explore your parents' situation. Then

with that in mind, we'll suggest ways to make your life more pleasant.

Right now you should be aware that everyone in North America is an immigrant or a descendant of an immigrant. Even the Native Americans and the Eskimos came here from another continent. Some immigrants walked here, some swam, some sailed in ships, some drove, some flew. So whether you landed in New York, or Miami, or El Paso, or Vancouver, or Los Angeles, you represent a stage in immigration.

Immigration enabled the United States and Canada to attain their present importance in the world. You may be surprised to know that people like to boast about their immigrant roots. According to the generation phenomenon, facts that your generation tries to forget, the next generation tries to recapture. So one day your children may be boasting about you. It would not even be too unusual if you yourself, years from now, were moved to boast about how your parents fared and your own struggles as an immigrant. To help you appreciate the role of immigration, later chapters present facts about the past and present.

Coping with immigrant parents is a problem that has been with us for generations. Henry Kissinger and Isaac Asimov were children when their parents brought them from Europe. Today both are highly successful Americans.

Henry Kissinger, diplomat and winner of the 1973 Nobel Prize for Peace, came here from Germany as a teenager. The family was fleeing Nazi persecution. Kissinger served in the ranks in the U.S. Army during World War II. After receiving a PhD in government, he joined the faculty of Harvard University. He became the chief architect of foreign policy for Presidents Richard M.

Henry Alfred Kissinger (State Department photo).

Isaac Asimov (Kurt Muller photo).

Nixon and Gerald R. Ford. He was the first naturalized American to become Secretary of State. Noted for his negotiating ability, Kissinger was active in initiating the first Strategic Arms Limitations Treaty with the then

Soviet Union. He also played a leading role in Nixon's visit to the People's Republic of China.

Isaac Asimov was a noted writer, scientist, and futurist. At the age of three he arrived at Ellis Island with a case of measles. His father and mother had left Russia in quest of a better life. After serving in the ranks in the Army in World War II, Asimov obtained a PhD in chemistry. Later he became a full-time writer, producing literally hundreds of popular books. His subjects include science fiction, pure science, literature, Shakespeare, history, and the Bible. He has even written mysteries and is good at composing limericks. He was the recipient of many awards for his writing.

CHAPTER 2

What Your Parents Left

And how can man die better
  Than facing fearful odds
For the ashes of his fathers
  And the temples of his gods?
                    —Thomas B. Macaulay, 1800–1859

Your parents had various reasons for coming to America*. To reunite a family is a usual one. This happens when an immigrant is later joined by a spouse and children. Your mother and father may have been fleeing civil war or revolution or religious persecution or an oppressive government or even genocide.

---

*America in most cases throughout this book refers to both Canada and the United States. Freda Hawkins in *Canada and Immigration* writes: "The more I have seen of the immigration process in different political environments, the more convinced I am that immigration, in nearly all its aspects, is a common experience for individuals and governments."

9

Some parents are here because their skills are particularly needed. Others perhaps fled famine or economic upheaval.

Whatever their reason for coming, they firmly believed they had arrived in a free country with no class barriers, a country where good education was provided for their children, a country where it was possible for anyone to be successful. That belief had sustained them through heartbreak and sometimes through perilous journeys and long stays in refugee camps. To emigrants from places such as Hong Kong and Vietnam the waiting periods may have seemed like never-ending prison terms.

Immigrant status may be classified technically as political, or refugee, and economic. The 1951 Geneva Convention of Refugees defines a refugee as any uprooted person who has "a well-founded fear of persecution for reasons of race, religion, nationality, membership in a particular social group, or political opinion." Cubans who escaped Fidel Castro by coming to the United States would be called refugees. Most of the "boat people" from Vietnam, Laos, and Cambodia as well as the Chinese students who were involved in the Tiananmen Square incident would also have this classification. Cambodians forbidden by the Khmer Rouge to practice Buddhism could qualify for political asylum. On the other hand, Mexicans leaving their country because opportunities for advancement are scarce have the status of economic emigrants. Actually it is often difficult to make a clear division between the two groups; sometimes the takeover of a totalitarian regime brings about economic collapse. The division is important, however, because refugees often gain entry whereas emigrants, even those with serious economic problems, may be refused.

Refugees cannot return to their native land while the

forces that caused them to leave are still in power. Such a situation would naturally be distressing to immigrant parents. Just knowing that return is possible can be cause for hope. But if that hope never existed or is taken away, refugees may become depressed or perhaps develop emotional problems. Feelings of guilt because an immigrant is a survivor rather than one who perished may become intense and add to depression.

Countless immigrants have expressed thanks for the opportunity to enter Canada or the United States. Then they make it clear that home to them is still Nicaragua, Afghanistan, Haiti—wherever. The lines quoted at the beginning of this chapter imply that the poet remained throughout his life in the place where he was born. For many that is possible and ideal. But for many others the bitterness of leaving home becomes a necessity. (It was once not uncommon for Chinese immigrants to provide for their ashes to be returned to their homeland.)

By the time you are parents yourselves, you too may have developed a deep attachment to the country that has been home to you, despite whatever you may have suffered within its borders.

Your parents' departure to a new country may have cut them off, though perhaps only temporarily, from their own parents and others to whom they once turned for advice and support. Mark Mathabane, a South African, noted in *Kaffir Boy in America* that immigrants also lack extended families. An extended family includes brothers- and sisters-in-law, aunts and uncles, and the like. In some cultures neighbors become substitute parents if necessary. In a strange land it takes time to make new friends, so immigrant parents cannot always depend on such support. Sometimes it is even difficult to find the solace of a familiar religion.

If your parents insist on celebrating their ethnic holidays—for instance, Japanese or Chinese New Year—instead of the Fourth of July, it is not surprising. That may be a way to counteract the isolation that they feel.

Feelings of isolation among immigrants are not new. The Pilgrims, who were largely responsible for making English culture dominant in the United States, arrived in the New World in 1620. William Bradford, who was to become their leader, wrote this about the band that had sailed with him in the *Mayflower*:

". . . they had now no friends to welcome them nor inns to entertain or refresh their weather-beaten bodies; no houses or much less towns to repair to, to seek for succour. . . . If they looked behind them, there was the mighty ocean which they had passed and was now as a main bar and gulf to separate them from all the civil [civilized] parts of the world. . . . What could now sustain them but the Spirit of God and His grace? May not and ought not the children of these fathers rightly say, 'Our fathers were Englishmen which came over this great ocean, and were ready to perish in this wilderness, but they cried unto the Lord, and He heard their voice and looked on their adversity.'"

Groups and individuals that act as sponsors sometimes add to immigrants' isolation by placing families at great distances from one another. It is generally agreed that newcomers, at first anyway, prefer to live among their own people in somewhat familiar surroundings. Some Vietnamese, for example, find the Gulf coast of Texas, Louisiana, Mississippi, and Florida attractive. They are

used to the climate and can find compatible work in seafood processing plants or on shrimp boats.

However, columnist Ben Wattenberg, in an article in *The Mining Journal* (July 1, 1989), warned of the dangers inherent in keeping large groups of immigrants from the same country geographically isolated within the United States. He wrote:

"Our people come from everywhere, but they are not organized as nations. Suppose when the English began coming to America in the 17th century, they all decided to come only to New England, to all stay there, and not allow anyone else in. Suppose the Germans did the same in Pennsylvania. Under this scenario, New York becomes all Jewish, Texas all Hispanic, California all Japanese and Nevada all Basque. Illinois? All Polish. Michigan? Only Arabs. Georgia? Exclusively Afro-American. But, instead, we got all mixed up. Call it geographic pluralism."

Most immigrants come to urban areas beset with problems totally unfamiliar to them. The Afghan may remember with appreciation his beautiful mountains, the Lao may recall with fondness his green rice fields, while both can see only the squalid side of the city.

Adapting has been particularly difficult for the Hmong, refugees from Laos who are tribal mountain dwellers. Spencer Sherman, author of "The Hmong in America" (*National Geographic*, October 1988), wrote:

"Since 1984 I have watched the Hmong adjust to life in the United States, seen the smallest of their tribal customs clash with American ways and often with U.S. laws. I have seen newly arrived Hmong ponder

the use of stoves and refrigerators, and young Hmong spike their hair and wear chains in styles that they see on television. I have seen elderly Hmong depressed over their loss of authority, and illiterate working-age men puzzle over the tools of the industrial revolution as the rest of America marches into the computer age."

One Hmong thought he was obliged to buy something each time he went into a store. Skills important in farming are not usually needed in urban areas, and the newcomer is often forced into an unskilled job at the minimum wage.

Immigrants come with a wide variety of skills; many are highly educated and experienced in their fields. But even for these persons, living in a city as competitive as New York or Los Angeles involves considerable stress.

What is known as culture shock varies in degree among immigrants. One problem that most encounter is that in America parents are less authoritarian than in most other countries. Related to this is the fact that most cultures respect their aged in the light of their extensive life experiences. In contrast, Americans consider their young more important than their old. Making this situation more difficult may be a son's or daughter's knowledge of English. That knowledge confers a certain amount of power if the parents have to depend on it. And parents may resent that power.

In many cultures most of the authority resides with the male. In other words, the men are macho, and it is accepted that women bear many children and stay at home to rear them. In America it may be necessary or desirable for the mother to work outside the home. A macho husband may resent that. Certainly his self-

esteem would suffer if his wife found work before he did—and that may well happen.

To exemplify, a recent study by John Sorenson, reported in *The Journal of Ethnic Studies,* Spring 1991, notes that Ethiopian men complain that the women, since coming to Canada, no longer follow the culture they were born into, but are influenced by feminist thinking. (See Chapter 13.)

Another illustration is given by author Joann Lee in *Asian American Experience in the United States.* She quotes a social worker: "I get a lot of complaints from parents. They say they come to this country to give their children the chance for a better education, but now they lose their children. This is the culture shock. The children now think they are free to do anything they want." The social worker went on to explain that when a mother asked her daughter about a phone number written in her notebook, the girl replied, "This is the child abuse number. My teacher told me that if you beat me I should call this number. You have no right to beat me. You will be fined; you will be imprisoned." The mother felt that she had lost the right to control her children, and lengthy explanations were needed to reassure her.

Parents escaping from a totalitarian regime may actually experience difficulty in adapting to the freedom found in America. Immigrants who lived, for example, under the oppression practiced in the former Soviet Union nevertheless did not have to make their own decisions about earning a living, educating their children, obtaining medical care, and so on. The government provided all this, and the citizen accepted it without question, the good with the bad. A Hmong new to these shores found his freedom "overwhelming."

James Tollefson, in *Alien Winds: The Reeducation of America's Indochinese Refugees,* makes a telling comment about unfamiliar food: "Sponsors buy hot dogs at baseball games for newly arrived refugees, or try to teach them how to cook hamburgers, when most refugees want to find an Asian store where they can find more familiar foods." The Armenian may yearn for shish kebab, the Cuban for rice and beans. The native of Vietnam likes quail eggs. The Mexican wants a tortilla. The Jamaican looks for curried chicken and allspice. A South African used to pap (porridge made from cornmeal), greens, and brown bread has trouble digesting all the fat present in the American diet. And so it goes. Your parents may never develop a taste for hamburgers and fries.

It is to be expected that your father and mother will cling to their native language, the language that has served them so well for so long. Yet there is little doubt that failure to speak and write the common language of the adopted country is a bar to advancement.

Teachers have long recognized that the young learn a new language faster than the old. That puts you at an advantage over your parents (assuming, of course, that they are not fluent in English or French). Then too, it is likely that you are more exposed to the new language and therefore have a better opportunity to become proficient in it.

Probably bilingualism is ideal for an immigrant family. (That does not imply that official bilingualism for a country should be encouraged.) At this point in your life, you may not care whether or not you are fluent in your parents' tongue, but that may change as you get older.

In time you may agree with a certain university professor who regrets that he did not learn Russian from his

father or grandparents. He was so intent on learning English well that he made no attempt to improve the little Russian he did know, so he gradually forgot it. By the time he wanted to learn the language of his heritage, his father and grandparents were dead.

Hispanics feel strongly that their language must not be forgotten because of immigration and are generally in favor of bilingual education. Some people believe that in time English and Spanish will be spoken in the United States as English and French are now spoken in Canada.

Although the problem is not too common, some highly trained and skilled immigrants actually lower their economic and professional status when they come to America. An example would be a physician established and successful in his homeland who works in his adopted country as a taxi driver. Usually such downward mobility occurs because licensing requirements of the new country have not been met. Sometimes positions are not available. With time, the licensing requirements can be met. But in the meantime the situation is a blow to the immigrant's pride as well as a serious economic hardship to him and his family.

This has been an overview of what your parents may have lost by coming to a new land. Fortunately, you are unlikely to experience many of their problems.

CHAPTER 3

What Your Parents Found— Expectations versus Reality

We don't have to worry about war and corruption any more. I'm willing to wash dishes or be a laborer—anything to get my family settled.

—Refugee from Vietnam, 1975

Despite whatever obstacles intervened, your parents managed to get themselves here. However, generations of immigrants have soon found that the streets of New York are not paved with gold, and that the "Gold Mountain" dream of some Asians is a delusion. In other words, the conditions the

newcomers found were often very different from what they had envisaged. Jonathan Raban, author of *Hunting Mr. Heartbreak: A Discovery of America*, notes that immigrants to America still arrive armed with fictions.

Some remain disillusioned. Joann Lee's book quotes Charles Ryu, a thirty-year-old Korean who arrived in the United States when he was seventeen:

> "The biggest disillusionment I had was that the American dream is a lie. It had a lot to do with growing up. As a kid you tended to see things in black and white. Now you see things in perspective. I did become an American citizen because I transplanted myself here. But all the promises of America are more of a dream and well-orchestrated hoax than reality—for most Americans, even. America is not a freedom-defending democratic country, but simply a capitalistic imperial force. . . . Still, a lot of other Koreans continue to come to America with the hope of making it in the American dream, which they couldn't do in Korea."

From the time of an immigrant's arrival, the language barrier is clear. As far back as 1814, De Witt Clinton observed that "the triumph and adoption of the English language has been the principal means of melting us down to one people." Clinton was a forward-looking man of his day and is remembered for his part in making a reality the Erie Canal, connecting the Hudson River with the Great Lakes.

More than a century and a half after Clinton, a teacher of immigrant children had this to say: "English is the great prohibitor. Without it, you can't advance, even if

you are otherwise qualified." In 1991 an authority on the use of English in the U.S. noted: ". . . it's indisputable that by not knowing how to read, write, speak or understand English in an English-speaking country, newcomers are condemned to a lifetime of poverty, injustice, and discrimination."

Your parents no doubt recognize that painful truth but perhaps have not become fluent in a language that is to them a foreign tongue. (A Chinese immigrant reports that his accent was equated with stupidity. Another immigrant notes that voices are raised when addressing a person with normal hearing but who is struggling with English.)

It is a fact of life that everyone encounters discrimination of one form or another, some persons meeting with it more frequently than others. Strange as it may seem, immigrants often face discrimination from others who are themselves immigrants or have closely related immigrant forebears. Sharon Pratt Kelly, the mayor of Washington, D.C., has observed: "It's always amazing that every group that's been discriminated against [can do] the same things towards someone else."

The history of the United States provides numerous examples of ethnic discrimination, some of which we shall present here.

When the Civil War ended in 1865, there were few railroad tracks west of the Mississippi River. Despite the difficulty of the terrain, extremes of weather, and threat of Indian attack, within four years tracks were laid between San Francisco and Omaha. This great feat was due largely to the efforts of immigrant labor. Irishmen employed by the Union Pacific Railroad worked westward from Nebraska, while the Central Pacific's workforce, about 90 percent Chinese, moved the project eastward from California. The linking of the two railways, cel-

ebrated with the driving of a golden spike, took place at Promontory Point in Utah in 1869. It was noted that in digging the tunnel through the Donnor Summit in the Sierra Nevada Mountains, the Chinese laborers cut more rock in a week than did the celebrated miners of Cornwall, England.

Most Chinese laborers in the late nineteenth century were single men or men whose wives were left at home. This situation suited the interests of the United States when a mobile workforce was needed both in the construction industry and for the harvesting of crops. At the same time, it was favored by many Chinese; according to the "hostage theory," women left in the home country assured that their husbands would send back money and eventually return. (Hawaii, on the other hand, encouraged the immigration of wives. The planters who raised sugarcane and rice knew that the men would be happier—also that the women would be an added source of labor, but at $3 per month instead of the $4 paid a man.)

The accomplishments of the Irish and the Chinese did not, however, save them from discrimination.

One of the reasons for prejudice against the Irish was that they were Roman Catholics in a predominantly Protestant nation.

The Orientals' steadfastness did not make them popular with American workers, who considered them inferior people willing to work for very low wages. Agitation started in California, which passed a law in 1887 ending Chinese immigration. Three years later the United States Congress passed an act that barred Chinese from entry to the country and barred Chinese aliens, or noncitizens, already in the country from citizenship. In the late 1890s arose a groundless scare, first voiced in

Germany, that the yellow races of China and Japan would increase in population and overrun areas occupied by whites. People who believed this referred to the Chinese as the Yellow Peril. Reenactments of the Chinese Exclusion Law were in effect until 1943.

Before 1910, Asians arriving in San Francisco were detained for questioning in a rude waterfront shed. Pressure from Chinese community leaders prompted the Bureau of Immigration to build a Pacific coast counterpart of Ellis Island (see page 94). Named Angel Island Immigration Station, it served for thirty years as a port of entry—or of deportation—for thousands of immigrants from Asia. It was isolated and grim, and the detainees were virtually held prisoner, sometimes for considerable periods of time. In recent years poems written on the walls have been translated; some of them express the writers' fears, despair, and desolation.

Obviously some of the discrimination against the Chinese arose because of their nonwhite skin. This discrimination extended to Japanese and Filipinos also.

Fearing the spread of Christianity and western authority, Japan had for many years shut out foreigners. Until 1886, Japanese were forbidden to leave their country. Once permitted to go abroad, numbers of them settled in California. With their extensive knowledge of farming, they were soon reclaiming swamplands and successfully raising fruits and vegetables.

But these Issei, as first-generation Japanese immigrants are called, were much resented by American farmers. When the San Francisco Board of Education ordered all Asians to attend segregated schools, the Japanese government protested.

To settle the matter, President Theodore Roosevelt made what is called a Gentlemen's Agreement—an

informal one with no legal standing. It was decided that there would be no segregated schools, and in turn Japan would limit the number of its emigrants.

Although a California Act of 1913 had barred non-citizens from buying land in that state, by 1919 about 74,000 Japanese owned land. They had got around the law by buying in the names of their American-born children, called Nisei. (Comparable to Nisei are Chicanos, the American-born children of Mexican parents.)

The Japanese, more than the Chinese, were now referred to as the Yellow Peril. A quote from *The Sacramento Bee*, a California newspaper, reflects some of the native feeling in 1921: "The intent on the part of the Japanese . . . now is to secure upon this continent a foothold for their race, not as individual units to be absorbed and assimilated in the great American melting pot, but as a compact body of loyal subjects of the Mikado. . . ." Some historians believe that the condescending and hostile attitude of the United States toward Japan played a part in prompting the surprise attack on Pearl Harbor in 1941.

With that bombing came hysteria, which amounts to uncontrollable fear or emotion. People became unnecessarily concerned about sabotage and espionage by the Japanese. Sabotage is destructive action carried on by enemy agents; espionage is another word for spying. No distinction was made between Japanese who immigrated to the United States—Issei—and native-born Nisei. Both often faced difficulties when they tried to buy food, cash checks, or even enter a hospital.

A few months later, both Issei and Nisei (the Japanese call the third generation Sansei and the fourth, Yonsei) living on the West Coast were ordered to leave. They were given crude housing in so-called internment camps

and relocation centers. All of these camps were in the desert or in Arkansas, places remote from the Pacific Coast, where it was feared that Japanese spies might learn of American naval operations. More than half of those interned were American citizens, yet some of them were detained for as long as three years. We know now that as a group they were remarkably loyal to the United States.

These people suffered great financial losses. Because they had very short notice before being removed, they sold many of their goods far below value. Often their crops were harvested by intruders who paid nothing. (California farmers were in favor of the relocation; it enabled them to gain Japanese-owned land.) Sometimes there was no time to sell a flourishing business, and of course no one to manage it for the absent owner. Only what could be carried by hand was allowed into the camps. Eventually the federal government granted some compensation, but it amounted to only about 10 cents on the dollar.

The United States' declaration of war on Japan applied to Germany and Italy also. However, Germans and Italians living in the country were not regarded as enemy aliens, as were the Japanese. Because of this, the World War II relocation action is considered a racist act.

By 1943 the War Department did allow Nisei from the camps and from Hawaii to volunteer. These men formed the 442nd Regimental Combat Team, a segregated unit that distinguished itself fighting in the European Theater. U.S. Senator Daniel Inouye of Hawaii fought with the 442nd and lost an arm in combat. Today the armed forces are integrated; units are composed of members of all races rather than being all white, all black, and so on.

In 1976 the federal government, represented by

President Gerald R. Ford, made a formal apology for the internments. In 1982 a federal commission recommended that each internee still living receive $20,000 as restitution. This was later paid.

The American Civil Liberties Union (ACLU) has described the relocation operation as "the greatest deprivation of civil liberties by government in this country since slavery." That is probably so, but under the stress of a war that turned out to be the greatest conflict of all time, most Americans were not aware of the inhumanity of the act.

During part of the time when entry of Chinese and Japanese was forbidden or restricted, Filipinos, who also have nonwhite skin, arrived in large numbers. In 1934, Congress declared the Philippines a commonwealth and promised full independence in 1946. The islands were also given the smallest immigration quota in existence— only 50 per year. Racists, labor leaders, and farmers who raised sugarcane or sugar beets supported independence for the Philippines because they knew it would be easier to exclude true foreigners (and, of course, their products) than to exclude people under the protection of the United States. Here we have an example of the basis of much discrimination—racism and also fear that the newcomers will cause economic hardship to those who have already established themselves.

Later we shall have more to say about immigration to Canada. We note now that there too the Japanese faced discrimination. Toward the end of the nineteenth century they settled largely in British Columbia and engaged in fishing, farming, and logging. But race riots occurred in Vancouver in 1907, and in 1942 Japanese were evacuated from the West Coast area to inland detention towns in an operation similar to the one in the United States.

Joann Lee tells of one internee, Henry Moritsugu. "I still feel there's a stigma attached to being Japanese because of what happened in the war," he told Mrs. Lee. "Today I consider myself a Canadian and not Japanese. My children's lives are totally Western." Once when Moritsugu was mistaken for a Chinese, someone countered that he was *Canadian*. "But underneath all that, there is prejudice there," Moritsugu observed.

Mrs. Lee points out a special type of discrimination described by Cao O, who immigrated from Vietnam in his teens: "No matter how many years I am here, even till the time I die, I will always speak English with an accent," he says. "That is a fact that I cannot deny. That is a fact that I cannot escape. And people will never see me as an American because the conventional wisdom is that if you are American, you should speak with no accent."

Discrimination was also practiced against people who had white skin but looked "different." Until the 1860s, 90 percent of the immigrants were from Central and Northern Europe. In general, they had some education and were Protestants. Because they were like most of the people already in the country, their assimilation was fairly rapid. By the 1890s, however, the pattern of immigration had changed, with most of the newcomers coming from Southern and Eastern Europe—Italians, Russians, Austrians, Hungarians, Croatians, and Bohemians. These people tended to have darker skin. Many were Catholics and Jews, and many were illiterate. Because they were unfamiliar, they were viewed with suspicion and not well accepted. Since many of them were poor, they were likely to work for low wages; that pleased employers but caused conflict with native workers, who looked to unions to improve their conditions.

Disturbed by the influx of the newer European immigrants, U.S. Senator Henry Cabot Lodge of Massachussetts asked, "What shall be done to protect our labor against this undue competition, and to guard our citizenship against an infusion which seems to threaten deterioration?" Lodge was the sponsor of legislation that denied admission of aliens who could not read. The measure passed Congress, to be vetoed by President William McKinley.

Although the supply of immigrant labor was very valuable to the progress of the nation, as more and more foreigners entered, even those who until recently had been foreigners themselves or whose parents had immigrated became apprehensive about the presence of so many aliens in their adopted country. Lines written in 1890 by the poet Thomas Bailey Aldrich express some of this resentment:

"Wide open and unguarded stand our gates,
And through them presses a wild motley throng—
Men from the Volga and the Tartar steppes,
Featureless figures of the Hoang-Ho,
Malayan, Scythian, Teuton, Kelt, and Slav,
Flying the Old World's poverty and scorn;
These bringing with them unknown gods and rites,—
Those, tiger passions, here to stretch their claws.
In street and alley what strange tongues are loud,
Accents of menace alien to our air,
Voices that once the Tower of Babel knew."

Unfortunately, the type of discrimination encountered by the Central Europeans is still with us. In 1989, National Public Radio reported on discrimination against some Pakistanis who had settled in Hudson County, New

Jersey. A local person was quoted as saying the Pakistanis looked "different."

It has been suggested that in general the only groups not well integrated by the second generation are those of a different color.

Sometimes discrimination may arise unexpectedly. Historically, the Germans were generally considered valuable and welcome immigrants. During World War I, however, when German-Americans resisted participation in a conflict with their native land they experienced serious prejudice. Feelings ran so high and became so absurd that sauerkraut was renamed liberty cabbage. In more recent times, some Iraqis living in Detroit experienced hostility during Operation Desert Storm.

Discrimination enters into many facets of everyday living. Despite laws, ways are found by unscrupulous persons to deny good jobs, decent housing, college entrance, club membership, and so on to worthy applicants. Parents of minority races are known to try to protect their children from the cruelty of discrimination, so your parents may have shielded you when you were unaware of it. Discrimination will always be with us, and it is not likely that you will be spared. It should lessen as we learn to understand one another better.

Note the quotation from the Vietnamese refugee at the beginning of this chapter. There is certainly no shame in washing dishes or operating a dishwasher, but it pays only the minimum wage, in turn forcing a family to live very frugally. With rents sky high, especially in cities, the family may well be forced to live in cramped, unattractive quarters, perhaps in a section where crime and drug abuse are rampant, causing tenants to live in fear.

Although your parents took it for granted that em-

ployment was available, sometimes that is not the case. And the reason or reasons may have nothing to do with the immigrant's ability or desire to work. For example, transportation may be the roadblock because there is not yet a family car; or layoffs may occur that in no way reflect an individual's work effort.

Even the weather may add to an immigrant's discomfort; a Lao or an Asian Indian who has never seen snow may find the winter in Minneapolis or Montreal distasteful.

In a new environment, cut off from family support and familiar faces and ways, your parents may feel duty-bound to ensure their control over your life in this new environment, which they do not altogether understand and of which they probably do not approve. At the same time, you notice that American teenagers are assertive and independent, and you want to be like them. That is only natural, but try to understand your parents' concerns.

Some parents may have little time to consider matters that are very important to you. Mrs. Lee interviewed Sam Sure, born in the United States of Chinese parents. Here is his view:

> "One common thread that runs through many Asian lives is that parents spend so much time working for the future of their children, that they don't devote enough time to their emotional needs. Either the parents are working and can't be there, or if they are at home, they are so tired they can't devote themselves to the children."

We all want to "belong," to be accepted. Your parents may even have adjusted well to American life but are not

Dr. An Wang emigrated from China when he was 25. By 28 he had earned a Ph.D. in physics from Harvard and invented a key element in computer memory. Using traditional Confucian values, he began Wang Laboratories, a highly successful, billion-dollar computer company.

yet accepted by native-born people. Youth is flexible, so this type of acceptance will probably not be a problem in your life. Whether it remains a problem for immigrant parents depends on individual characteristics—some sixty-year-olds are more flexible than some twenty-year-olds, but that is rare. It has been stated that for the *adult* immigrant complete assimilation into a new culture is probably impossible. If it is impossible in your family, try to accept the fact with understanding.

CHAPTER 4

Coping with Your
Situation

No one can make you feel inferior without your consent.
—Eleanor Roosevelt, 1884–1962

Psychologists agree that good communication among family members does much to ease tension. For various reasons, however, many families communicate poorly among themselves.

The members of the generation that preceded you, especially those from a non-American background, are somewhat inclined to keep their thoughts to themselves. Besides that, your parents may have an Old World attitude that says in effect, "I am in authority. You do as I say without questions."

Young persons are usually less inhibited than their elders and are more likely to express their desires and displeasures. Americans are prone to analyze their thoughts and let them be known. You may tend to do that, but not to the extent that you are ready to discuss them with your parents.

If you find that communication is poor between you and your parents, tell them in a respectful way that you would like to know their views on an issue and that you want them to understand why you feel as you do about it. Choosing an appropriate time to say this is important. You are not likely to get much cooperation if you approach the subject when a family crisis is demanding your parents' attention.

Earning money yourself can do much to improve your situation. Also, it will introduce you to the work world in which you must compete—a world that is different from family and school. It is essential that such work not interfere with your academic performance; after all, a good education is very high on your parents' list of priorities and probably on yours too.

Is work available? Most high schoolers can find suitable part-time jobs during the school year. Regulations pertaining to the labor of minors vary. A work permit is usually required and can be obtained through school authorities. (A minor son or daughter is permitted to work in a family business without restrictions.) In the United States employers are not required to pay minors the minimum wage.

The jobs available to you will in general require little training. When training is required, it is given "on the job." In any job, employers value honesty, reliability, and industry. Coming late to work and presenting a sloppy appearance do not endear one to the boss.

The two stories that follow show that a part-time job may have unexpected benefits.

During her high school years Lillian took a job as baby-sitter for a woman with unusual insight. Very soon they

both realized that Lillian, though competent and reliable, was too impatient with children to enter a profession such as elementary school teaching. The employer had noticed that the high schooler was interested in flowers and made attractive arrangements with great ease. She suggested a course in flower arranging, which Lillian took. It was a great idea; the former baby-sitter ultimately opened her own flower shop, which became a successful enterprise.

Ten-year-old Larry took on a paper route. Within six months he had sold more subscriptions than any of his predecessors had over a period of years. By the time Larry was a freshman in high school, the paper route was adding substantially to his growing bank account. Long before graduation, he had decided that salesmanship was his strong point. He became a successful salesman, always enjoying his ability to talk people into buying things he thought they needed.

Summer jobs are hard to come by. Employers complain that just about the time a new employee learns the job, fall comes and it's time for the student to return to school. But you might be fortunate enough to find a job you could hold on to for a few successive summers. Or you might have an experience similar to Gino's. An Italian-American who had no ambition to go to college, Gino took a summer job that required menial work on an assembly line. The experience made him realize that education could lead to increased earnings and more meaningful work. After a long struggle, he obtained a PhD and became a professor.

If your father and mother need instruction in English,

you should make every effort to encourage that. Not being fluent in the language adds to their isolation and frustration.

Classes in English are provided under the auspices of a variety of agencies. For instance, as many as 300 adults from 40 nations have enrolled in the International English Center, a program sponsored by the Grand Rapids, Michigan, school district. (Their children attended special classes at regular schools.)

Sometimes volunteers provide individual tutoring. Unlike programs that are aimed mainly at improving an immigrant's English, the Boston area's One with One provides assistance that enables a newcomer to become proficient in whatever area he or she chooses. That means that each volunteer tutor "custom-fits" the language instruction to meet the needs and desires of the student.

Regardless of what system your parents enroll in, you can be a great help if they are wrestling with the complexities of a new language. Don't be impatient with them, and don't be arrogant, even if you think they are very slow.

Some young people enjoy keeping a journal; it is an opportunity to produce something unique, something personal. If you feel frustrated and angry, perhaps *writing* your thoughts, rather than *blurting* them out, may help. Try it for a month or so to see how it works. If you do not want others to know your feelings, keep what you have written out of sight. Just putting your thoughts on paper may make you feel better. In any case, it is good practice in expressing yourself.

Telling your troubles to a close friend or acquaintance can be beneficial to you. If you do it too frequently, however, you may bore your confidant and break up a good relationship.

Professional counseling has helped many people. A counselor is trained to listen and, in an unbiased way, to help you come to your own decision about solving a problem. The schools have counselors to guide you. Priests, rabbis, and other religious leaders are also equipped to help and are used to dealing with families as a whole. If you feel that this kind of professional help would benefit you, seek it without delay.

The schools offer many extracurricular activities such as sports, music, photography, debate, journalism. If you do not work, one of these fields might interest you. It would also provide time away from home and opportunity to make new friends.

Most school libraries have the Coping series put out by The Rosen Publishing Group to which this book belongs. Get acquainted with all the titles. Some, for example, *Coping with Family Stress*, might be of help. A list of handbooks is given at the end of the chapter. They are available at most public libraries.

Public libraries are sources of almost limitless information, thanks largely to computers. First and foremost, libraries provide access to great literature. Once you become a reader, you can escape to a new world from which you can derive much pleasure and benefit. Second, libraries can provide materials to guide you on practical points such as career choices, employment statistics, naturalization, and the like. Get to know the reference librarians and other personnel at your local library. They will direct you about how best to use the vast resources that are open to you. Third, libraries supply video and audiotapes, paintings, and such, and often offer interesting cultural programs.

The United States and Canada are blessed with scores of agencies that may be able to assist you. The Red Cross,

Andrew Carnegie. Carnegie emigrated from Scotland at the age of 12 and immediately want to work as a bobbin boy in a textile factory. His business acumen and organizational ability made him a millionaire. A man without formal education, he never forgot the enjoyment libraries had provided him, and he donated much of his fortune for the establishment of free public libraries (courtesy Carnegie Mellon University).

for example, offers courses in water safety, cardiopul-
monary resuscitation (CPR), and baby-sitting. The list
below gives the names of agencies and organizations
equipped to deal with some of the problems encountered
by immigrant families. The services provided vary from
place to place, but it is worth a phone call to find out
about the local branch or division.

When you are feeling down, remember the words of
Eleanor Roosevelt at the beginning of this chapter. If you
don't know about that great lady, go to your public library
and look her up. The time will be well spent.

Agencies in the United States

If an address is not given, look up the local unit in your phone
book.

Alcoholics Anonymous (AA)

American Red Cross

American Refugee Commission
2344 Nicollet Avenue
Minneapolis, MN 55404

Big Brothers/Big Sisters of America

Boy Scouts

Buddhist Council for Refugee Rescue and Resettlement
800 Sacramento Street
San Francisco, CA 94108

Catholic Social Services

Girl Scouts

Lutheran Immigration and Refugee Service
390 Park Avenue South
New York, NY 10016

National Center for Urban Ethnic Affairs (NCUEA)
P.O. Box 20, Cardinal Station
Washington, D.C. 20064

National Coalition of Advocates for Students
100 Boylston Street, Suite 737
Boston, MA 02116-4610

New York Association for New Americans
730 Broadway
New York, NY 10003

Planned Parenthood Federation of America

Puerto Rican Family Institute
116 West 114th Street
New York, NY 10025

Vietnam Refugee Fund
6433 Northern Drive
Springfield, VA 22150

Young Men's Christian Association (YMCA)

Young Women's Christian Association of U.S.A. (YWCA)

United Way

Canadian Agencies

Affiliation of Multicultural Societies and Services of British
    Columbia
1254 West 7th Avenue
Vancouver, BC V6H 186

Alcoholics Anonymous (AA)

Al-Anon Family Groups
P.O. Box 6433, Station J
Ottawa, ON K2A 3Y6

Association of Parent Support Groups in Ontario
11 Nevada Avenue
Willowdale, ON M2M 3N9

Big Brothers/Big Sisters

Boy Scouts

Canadian Association of Neighbourhood Services (CANS)
3102 Main Street
Vancouver, BC V5T 3G7

Canadian Institute on Minority Rights
4404 St. Dominique
Montreal, PQ H2W 283

Canadian Red Cross Society

Esperanto Youth of Canada
P.O. Box 126, P.O. Box Beaubien
Montreal, PQ H2G 3CB

Family Service Canada

Girl Guides

Jewish Immigrant Aid Service of Canada
4600 Bathurst Street
Willowdale, ON M2R 3V3

Muslim Education and Welfare Foundation of Canada
2580 McGill Street
Vancouver, BC V5K 1H1

Ontario Council of Agencies Serving Immigrants
579 St. Clair Avenue
West Toronto, ON M6C 1A3

Planned Parenthood Federation of Canada

United Way

Useful Handbooks

Canadian Almanac and Directory (current year). Toronto: Canadian Almanac and Directory Publishing Company.

Seely, Margaret. *Handbook for Citizenship*, 2nd ed. Hayward, CA: Alemany Press, 1989.

World Almanac and Book of Facts (current year). New York: Pharos.

CHAPTER 5

Your Generation

> . . . dreaming and wishing for a better life in this new land was the easy part; but having to start a new life all over again, that was the hard part.
>
> —Veve Insisiengmay as a junior in high school

During the 1980s an educator named Margaret Gibson made a careful study of immigrant students at a high school in California's Sacramento Valley. These students were the children of Punjabi Sikhs from northwest India, and the great majority of them were born abroad. Dr. Gibson's findings seem in a general way to parallel the experiences of other foreign-born immigrant children. Both generations— parents and children—found prejudice in the community.

These Punjabis, whether themselves educated or not, stressed education and expected their children to be trained for a specific profession or occupation. Daughters, however, were steered toward secretarial work or jobs as bank tellers and the like that do not require long preparation. Obtaining a college degree was not en- couraged because a young woman was expected to marry

soon, her husband preferably a recent arrival from the Punjab. Parents tended to assume that academic success comes more from hard work than innate ability or prior advantages. No great weight was given to extracurricular activities.

The immigrant mothers and fathers were aware that their offspring were less tied to Asian Indian customs and values than they themselves, but some still expected their adolescent children to turn to them for direction and approval. Especially frowned upon was the American custom of letting young people decide important matters on their own. One parent complained, "He does not listen to anyone, does everything as he pleases—the way the Americans do. To us that is not right." Parental decisions included choosing mates for their children; marriage was seen as the union of two families rather than two individuals.

The older generation opposed any attempt of their children to assimilate into the new culture by turning their backs on their native culture: ". . . they will be neither like us nor like them. . . . We can never be like them, nor do we need to . . . the most important thing for the children is to receive a good education. Through education they will be recognized and respected."

Mixing socially with American students was discouraged; Americanization promoted undesirable characteristics such as individualism and independence.

Attitudes and beliefs like these naturally caused intergenerational conflict. The girls in particular felt pulled in two directions because the message of the new culture stressed independence, decision-making, university education, postponement of marriage and children to advance a career—and so on. One girl complained:

"My parents don't like my clothes, my hair, the way I talk. They don't like my future plans. They don't like anything about me. They don't like my philosophy about marriage. . . . [They] say, 'Don't talk to anybody; don't go anywhere; come straight home.' . . . I don't know how I can get it through their heads that I want to go out with a guy if they won't even let me go out with a girl."

The following should be encouraging: Data obtained later by Dr. Gibson showed that most of the girls *did* go to college. Some of them married young men *not* raised in India. And after marriage, conflict with the parents diminished.

Older brothers and sisters of the Punjabi students seemed to have the desire to acculturate but not to assimilate. Said one, "I think you are richer because you are exposed to two cultures and you can pick the best from both. You have to make an adjustment, but I wouldn't choose it any other way."

Madelin Tallez is one of the subjects interviewed by Marilyn Davis for her book *Mexican Voices—American Dreams*. At the time, Madelin was a junior high school student in Oceanside, California. Her mother had brought her from Mexico the year before. The school offered classes in English and Spanish and she was enjoying PE, which was not open to girls in Mexico. She missed eating mangoes and being able to pick fruit off the trees. But her mother cooked Mexican food for the family. Madelin told author Davis, "If I had a friend who was coming to the United States, I would tell them to put a lot of effort into learning English, because some words are very difficult.

"When I grow up I want to stay here and work in a

career until I earn enough money; then I want to go back to Mexico."

Lily Truong was born in Vietnam. She immigrated first to Canada and came to the United States in 1989. She speaks Chinese, Vietnamese, and English and considers herself a creative person with a positive attitude; she likes drawing and singing. She found learning English difficult; also adapting to a new life-style. After graduation from Aurora Central High in Colorado, she intends to go to college. Lily believes that immigrant students should make every effort to go to college.

Another Vietnamese who has settled in Colorado is Vu Ngruyen. He is from Saigon City but was in the Philippines before coming to the United States in 1989. Entering a new culture was not easy at first. Although he is having trouble mastering English, he hopes to go to college after graduation from Aurora Central High School. He is interested in music. Vu feels that a good knowledge of English is necessary to an immigrant student's success.

Vinson C. Ulep is now a sophomore at Marquette Senior High School in Michigan. His parents emigrated from the Philippines in 1971, before he was born. His father is a physician. Vinson's interests are drums, football, biking, and reading. He looks forward to obtaining a college degree and becoming a member of the lower-upper or upper-middle class. English is his native tongue, but he takes pride in the fact that he can converse in French with his older brother and sister. He has not

experienced racial prejudice or discrimination at school. He finds that in Marquette, where there are few immigrants, people seem especially interested in him because he comes from a different culture. Stories told by his parents have convinced him that America is a good place to live.

Moving to America was something positive in Veve Insisiengmay's life. She was born in Laos, but in the mid-1970s her father, Sengchanh, came to believe that he and his family were in danger from the Communist government that had taken over the country. He had worked in the United States and wanted to move his wife and four children there. First he devised a plan to get them safely to Thailand. What happened in that venture has been described in the news bulletin of the Wisconsin parish that finally sponsored the Insisiengmay family:

> "While trying to flee Laos, Sengchanh went to the immigration office to get permission to visit relatives in Thailand. Realizing that he wanted to get out of the country, the officials allowed him to leave, taking his wife and only *one child* with him. Knowing full well that he wouldn't go far with three of his children left behind, the officials granted him a three-day pass. Entry *into* Laos is allowed, and people from Thailand pass freely in and out of Laos. So with his wife and one child in Thailand, Sengchanh went back and paid Thai visitors to take each of his three children over the river as if they were their own. That evening after dark, Sengchanh swam the Mekong River to escape, hoping he would find all his family safely on the Thai side. They arrived

in Camp Ubol, the refugee camp in Thailand, on January 2, 1977.

During the year and a half that the family lived in a one-room bamboo hut in the camp, they slept on straw mats on the floor in crowded conditions. Bad sanitation and lack of water created health problems, for which there was only one doctor and three nurses available for the 19,000 people in the camp. One and a half cups of rice a day and occasionally a small portion of meat or fish was their total diet."

In the spring of 1979, thanks to sponsorship provided through Catholic Social Services, the family arrived in Wisconsin, where Sengchanh had a cousin.

Veve missed the diet she had been used to: "I remember having gone through a month without rice because there wasn't any Oriental store anywhere in Waukesha back then."

The children entered a six-week summer bilingual program, which had a weekly field trip.

Sengchanh spoke English well and almost immediately found a good job. His wife, Hongsavady, was trained as a veterinarian's assistant. However, she took a night class in English to become more fluent before she looked for work. When Veve first went to the third grade, the only words she knew were "hello" and "goodbye."

Her first winter in Wisconsin was "absolutely amazing." She had not heard the word "snow" until her cousins mentioned it. "I remember one time when I stayed up all night waiting for the first flakes to fall," she says, "and the next morning, when it did fall, I would sit at the window and stare at it all day. Somehow, I thought it was salt."

But she quickly became acclimated and toward the

end of that school year had "pretty much got the hang of everything."

Eight years later, as a student at Waukesha High School, she could say, "I am proud of myself because I worked very hard to get where I am now."

By 1991 she was enrolled as a junior at the University of Wisconsin, Madison. Her major is architecture.

Veve's dreams were fulfilled through perseverance and her positive attitude.

CHAPTER 6

You versus Your Parents

Youth is full of pleasure,
Age is full of care.

—Shakespeare

Young people are risk-takers, idealistic and often impulsive, but set on doing things their elders would hesitate to attempt.

This risk-taking is important to human progress. For instance, black students (and some white) played a major role in bringing about the reforms gained in civil rights during the 1960s. To cite another example, student demonstrations on college campuses against the Vietnam War had a strong influence in bringing about the withdrawal of American forces.

On the other hand, experience is an invaluable teacher. Your parents have experience that you lack. That accumulated experience makes them cautious and often

unwilling to take the risks that are common with your generation.

It was noted during World War II that young fighter pilots often made instant decisions that proved to be correct. Older pilots were inclined to think about the consequences and while doing so sometimes lost important opportunities. In the long run, some pilots lost their lives because of instant decisions, and some lost their lives because of hesitancy.

That brings home the fact that some of the time youth is correct, and some of the time age is correct. Usually it takes the passage of time to determine whether or not a given decision is a wise one.

As mentioned, adolescence is a trying time for both parents and their offspring. A high schooler is no longer a child; he or she is beginning to think like an adult, although not yet having adult responsibilities. The body has matured, with the sex hormones causing new feelings and desires, but emotional maturity has not been reached. At this time, the adolescent's "instant" solution to an important problem may well differ from that of parents, who know from past experience that satisfactory answers may require more time. These differing attitudes are bound to produce conflict, which is often reflected in confrontations between the generations.

What takes place naturally between parents and young adults is likely to be exaggerated when there is transplantation to a new culture, as occurs with immigration. We present here some fictionalized incidents representing types of arguments that are likely to occur.

Tuan (who rejected his name after he came to the United States and now calls himself Tim) wants to become an

auto mechanic. Last summer he watched a friend's father work on a car engine and became fascinated, asking numerous questions. Since then he has "talked cars" with Mr. Jones at every available opportunity. Mr. Jones is aware that Tim has found it very difficult to keep up in math. The truth is, he has not done well in any subject. In light of this, Mr. Jones suggested that Tim consider switching from his college course to vocational education.

Tim's father became angry when his son mentioned what he would like to do. The older man comes from a culture that respects learning, and he had assumed that his son would pursue an academic career. To the father's way of thinking, he knows what is best for his son and expects him to respect his parents, not argue with them. He did not consider that Tim should have a say in a decision affecting his future. Nor did it occur to him that perhaps Tim lacks the ability to do well in a rigorous academic course.

In a case such as this, the advice of a good vocational counselor could be helpful. It would be important to determine whether Tim's interest in car engines is a passing one or really serious, and whether he has been working to his limit in the college course or is not exerting himself sufficiently.

Mercedes is in love with an American boy whom she has been seeing without her mother's knowledge. She is not allowed to date, and it would make her mother still angrier if she knew that her daughter's boyfriend is not Hispanic.

Mercedes became ill at school one day and was sent to the school nurse. The nurse asked if there was a possibility that she could be pregnant. When Mercedes

said there was, the nurse sent her to a Planned Parenthood clinic for a pregnancy test. The test was negative, showing that she was not pregnant. A Planned Parenthood counselor then suggested that Mercedes should use some method of birth control. She pointed out that a condom would be a safeguard against both AIDS and pregnancy. Convinced that she would not contract AIDS from her boyfriend, Mercedes chose the pill.

A problem arose when her mother found the pills. Mrs. Perez's first reaction was disappointment in Mercedes; she felt that her daughter had deceived her. But she was also faced with a dilemma. For the past few years her great fear has been that Mercedes would become pregnant before marriage. That would be bad enough, but it would be unbearable if her daughter sought an abortion, as some American teenagers do. The pill would prevent pregnancy, but birth control is contrary to her religious beliefs.

Since Mercedes has no intention of giving up her boyfriend, she must tell her mother that she will continue to see him and at the same time assure her that she will take the birth control pills without fail. In time, the mother is likely to decide that the pill is better than an unwanted pregnancy.

Bill (he does not reveal the name given him by his parents) was born in the United States after his family immigrated to Detroit from Iraq. He speaks English without an accent and now works harder than ever to become Americanized. (He has not forgotten some of the taunts he endured during the Gulf War.) A short time ago he began to swim with some of his fellow students during a Friday evening open hour. He likes to swim, but it

is primarily a way to make new friends that have no connection with Iraq.

After the second week his father ordered him to drop the swimming and instead go to the home of a family friend who was giving a series of talks on Iraq. Bill suspects that his father's real purpose is to prevent him from becoming friendly with American classmates. Although he has complied with his father's orders, Bill's growing resentment has created an atmosphere of hostility in the household.

Bill's father is deliberately trying to isolate his son from some of the evils associated with the city—drugs, alcohol, violence, teenage pregnancy, and so on. Keeping his son away from American friends and acquaintances is a way to do that. At the same time, exposing the boy to Iraq's proud and ancient culture is a plus. To his way of thinking, a father deserves respect and obedience, and he is distressed by his son's attitude.

The father's intentions, although well meant, are unrealistic; he cannot isolate his son from the culture in which the family now lives. The father is also being unfair to most of Bill's classmates, who could well be good, rather than bad, influences.

The situation might improve if Bill could bring home an American classmate who represents the virtues admired by Bill's father and have the young man meet and talk with the father. Enlisting the help of the mother is another possibility.

John, the American-born son of a Chinese family, is a junior in high school. He has become a member of the drama club and is intensely interested in dramatics. The teacher in charge of the club suggested recently that

John major in theater when he goes to college. The idea appeals to John, but there was much consternation when he mentioned it at home.

His parents consider dramatics frivolous and would prefer that he devote the time to academics. However, they made no serious objections until he told them about his plans for college. His father cannot understand why his son is contemplating a career on the stage when he should be preparing himself for a professorship or at least to make a good living. Annoyed that an outsider had advised his son, he has ordered John to leave the drama club.

A compromise is possible: The father could agree to allow John to continue in the club so long as his grades do not suffer. Another suggestion: The father might revise his opinion of the value of dramatics if he could be persuaded to attend one of the club's productions.

Mun, fifteen, from Korea, has considerable musical talent. He has been taking violin lessons but recently became interested in the guitar through an American friend. Now he wants to drop the violin lessons and has suggested to his parents that the money thus saved would buy him an electric guitar. The suggestion immediately prompted an argument with his father.

Musical ability is highly prized by Mun's parents; they have secret aspirations for him to become concert master in one of the great American symphony orchestras. The idea that Mun forgo the opportunity they are affording him is unacceptable.

If Mun really wants an electric guitar, he could earn the money to buy it. That in itself would do much to convince his parents that he is serious about learning to

play it. Mastery of the violin and the theory of music that he is now gaining from his teacher are assets that will benefit him in any career choice that involves music.

Countless adults have expressed the wish that they had never given up music lessons when they were young. Countless adults have also noted that being forced to practice made them dislike music. The preferred course of action is difficult to determine, but it seems ill advised for Mun to drop his violin lessons at this time.

Naomi recently arrived from Russia. She is a first-class athlete, already the holder of a gold medal for figure skating, and she has placed in gymnastic contests. She is on her high school basketball team. Last week, practice hours for the girls' team were reduced to give the boys more time. Naomi's teammates are organizing all the female students in the school for a protest strike next Monday, but Naomi's mother has forbidden her daughter to participate. Naomi has accepted the decision without comment, but she is bitter about it because basketball means so much to her.

Despite her pride in Naomi's accomplishments, Mrs. Kaplan does not approve of youthful rebellion against authority. In her estimation, an edict from the school administration is to be obeyed, not resisted.

Naomi could help the tension between her mother and herself if she explained her side. She should persuade Mrs. Kaplan that women are legally entitled to the same rights as men, and that to preserve these rights women must let their voices be heard.

Won's family run a successful restaurant. Now sixteen, Won has worked there since he was twelve. This year, in

a graphic arts class, he found himself intrigued by how much can be done by computers in this field. Through his instructor he has been offered an after-school job in a quick print shop. His father and mother strongly oppose the idea and insist that he continue to work for them.

The parents assume that their children will stay indefinitely at the restaurant. The older two are there, so why should Won want to do differently? What is graphic arts, and how would it lead to anything productive?

The family's restaurant has progressed to the point that Won's help is no longer really necessary. His teacher knows that the experience gained in the print shop could be helpful to Won later. A possible solution would be to have the instructor explain to the parents the kind of work Won wants to do and the opportunities available in the field. Then he could tell them how the part-time job would be of benefit now—with earnings and experience that would count later.

In most situations some compromise is possible. Bear in mind that compromise means that each side concedes something. In other words, you must be prepared to give in to some degree in order to reach a settlement. Learning to compromise is part of growing up, and to do it gracefully is an accomplishment.

CHAPTER 7

The Flag—Symbol of Obligation

A patriotic American is never so proud of the great flag under which he lives as when it comes to mean to other people, as well as to himself, a symbol of hope and liberty.
—President Woodrow Wilson

Whether you were born a Canadian or an American citizen or whether you immigrated, Canada or the United States is entitled to your loyalty, or allegiance, as it is called. The flag, although only a piece of cloth, is a symbol of what that country represents, and it should therefore be treated with respect.

This chapter discusses the American flag itself and the pledge to it. Several stirring tributes have been written to the flag, but none surpasses Francis Scott Key's poem, "The Star Spangled Banner." The next time you sing or hear it, try to match the words to the story given later.

How the flag was designed is not clear. We do know

that in 1777 (one year after the colonies declared themselves independent of England) the Second Continental
Congress adopted this resolution:

> Resolved: that the flag of the United States be thirteen
> stripes, alternate red and white, and that the union
> be thirteen stars, white in a blue field, representing a
> new constellation.

The thirteen stars and stripes stood for the original
colonies that signed the Declaration of Independence. As
new states joined the union, new stars and stripes were
added. By 1818, however, it was realized that too many
stars and stripes would spoil the flag's design, and a law
was passed that only a new star would be added for
each new state. In 1912, by Executive Order of President
William Howard Taft, the relative proportions of the flag
and the arrangement of the stars were specified. The last

The United States flag in use today. It is sometimes called Old Glory
or the Stars and Stripes.

two stars—the 49th and 50th—were added in 1959 when
Alaska and Hawaii gained statehood. It was not until
July 4, 1960, under President Dwight D. Eisenhower,
that a banner with fifty stars became the official flag.

The Pledge of Allegiance is a century old. There was
controversy about its authorship, but it is now attributed
to Francis Bellamy, who died in 1931. Bellamy was a
member of the editorial staff of The Youth's Companion, a
popular magazine published in Boston. He was chairman
of a committee appointed to develop a program to celebrate the 400th anniversary of the discovery of America.
The pledge was published in The Youth's Companion
of September 8, 1892, and was recited at the World's
Columbian Exposition (similar to a world's fair) in Chicago
on October 21, 1892.

The original version was as follows: "I pledge allegiance
to my flag and to the Republic for which it stands, one
Nation indivisible, with liberty and justice for all."

Today in school you say, "I pledge allegiance to the flag
of the United States of America and the Republic for
which it stands, one Nation under God, indivisible, with
liberty and justice for all." In 1923 "my flag" was changed,
and in 1954 "under God" was inserted. The pledge gained
official sanction by Congress in 1945.

Francis Scott Key was a patriot, and his country's flag
meant a great deal to him. But he was opposed to the
War of 1812 (between the United States and England).
He was also aware that many of his countrymen hoped the
war would bring the conquest of Canada, which of course
was a British colony, and he said that he did not want to

fight "unoffending Canadians." However, the presence of British vessels off Maryland (his home state) changed his mind, and the year 1813 saw him in uniform.

In civilian life Key was a successful lawyer with a practice in Georgetown, District of Columbia, where he lived with his wife and children. After British forces burned the nation's Capitol on August 24, 1814, chaos reigned in the area around Washington.

Sometime during this period the British captured William Beanes, a doctor from Upper Marlborough. The reason is not clear. Although British officers had been quartered in Beanes's home and he had treated some of their wounded, the doctor was now a prisoner aboard a ship somewhere near the mouth of the Potomac River.

Key, temporarily freed from military duty in Georgetown when the British departed, was approached to obtain the release of his friend, Beanes. The lawyer first personally obtained President James Madison's sanction. He then rode to Annapolis to have General William Winder write a letter on behalf of Dr. Beanes, for presentation to General Robert Ross, commander of the British forces.

Around September 2, Key sailed from Baltimore in a small boat manned by a few sailors. He was accompanied by Colonel John Skinner, an American who was in charge of prisoners and accustomed to arranging prisoner exchanges. Skinner had obtained letters from wounded British officers stating that they were treated well by the Americans. Key and Skinner expected to find the British fleet at least 100 miles down Chesapeake Bay.

After three or four days, when they were near the mouth of the Patuxent River, Key's party sighted British naval vessels sailing up the bay toward Baltimore. Skinner hailed the *Tonnant*, flagship of the admiral, and he and Key were invited aboard.

After some hesitation, General Ross agreed to Beanes's release. The Americans were told that they would be detained until completion of the impending joint land and naval attack on Baltimore. This was to prevent their disclosing the plans of the British. With Beanes, they were transfered to the frigate *Surprize*, and their boat, with its sails removed, was towed. By September 11 the British vessels, numbering about forty, had reached North Point, at the mouth of the Patapsco River, some ten miles from Baltimore.

Early the next morning Key and the others were moved to their sailboat, made fast astern the *Surprize* and marked with a white flag. That night the fleet moved to a position about two miles below Fort McHenry, located at the entrance to Baltimore's inner harbor. The fear of running aground deterred a closer approach.

On the morning of September 13 the British bombardment began. It was to last for twenty-four hours and involve at least 1,500 bombs. The fort's light guns did not carry as far as the flagship, but Key was in a precarious position, even with the white flag of truce. In the midst of the smoke, while daylight lasted, Key could see with his telescope the fort's huge American flag. It had been made to order that summer by Mrs. Mary Young Pickersgill. One of the largest battle flags ever flown, it measured 42 by 30 feet, with alternate red and white stripes and fifteen stars for the original states plus Kentucky and Vermont.

During the rainy night Key paced the deck in the darkness. When the bombardment ceased he was not sure whether his countrymen had surrendered or whether the British had given up. When dawn came, he peered anxiously into his telescope to see which flag was flying over the fort, the American or the British. When to his

great relief he saw the former, he wrote the skeleton of a poem on the back of a letter he had in his pocket.

Historians today debate about the actual flag that Key saw. They wonder how such a very large flag, rain-soaked, could fly in the breeze. It is known that the fort owned a smaller "storm" flag; but would that have been visible eight miles away? Then in 1969 there came to light an account written in 1841 by Midshipman Robert Barrett of the British frigate *Hebrus*. The *Hebrus* was part of the squadron repulsed by the Americans. Barrett noted that as the British withdrew "a most supurb and splendid ensign" was raised at Fort McHenry. The hour, according to the ship's log, was about nine, not Key's dawn. Is it safe to rely on facts recorded so long after they occurred? We do not know. At any rate, Key saw the flag of his country flying from the fort, we are not sure when, and the sight inspired him to write an unforgettable poem.

Now back to the story. As the British prepared to withdraw, the sails of the little boat were returned and she was permitted to head upstream to the city wharves. That night at the Old Fountain Inn, Key completed his poem and made a clean copy. He was an amateur poet of long standing, and composition came easily. Reputed to be lacking in musical talent, he wrote his work to be sung to the tune of "To Anacreon in Heaven," an English drinking song by John Stafford Smith.

The next day Key showed his poem to Judge J.H. Nicholson, second in command at Fort McHenry and brother-in-law of Mrs. Key. Nicholson had it printed as "Defence of Fort M'Henry" without the name of the author. On September 20 the Baltimore *Patriot* ran it, and the following day it appeared in the Baltimore *American*. The *Patriot*'s editor termed it a "beautiful

and animated effusion which is destined to outlast the occasion. . . ." On January 6, 1815, the *National Intelligencer* recorded the title, "Star Spangled Banner." Whether Key so named his poem is not known.

The song grew in popularity. During the Spanish-American War, Admiral Dewey had it played at naval ceremonies. Later President Woodrow Wilson promoted it. Then in 1931 President Herbert Hoover signed an act making "The Star Spangled Banner" the national anthem of the United States. There is no official version, but the third stanza is now usually omitted.

Here it is:

The Star-Spangled Banner
By Francis Scott Key
(1780–1843)

O say, can you see, by the dawn's early light,
What so proudly we hailed at the twilight's last
  gleaming?
Whose broad stripes and bright stars, through the
  perilous fight,
O'er the ramparts we watched, were so gallantly
  streaming!
And the rockets' red glare, the bombs bursting in air,
Gave proof through the night that our flag was still
  there:
  O say, does that star-spangled banner yet wave
  O'er the land of the free and the home of the
  brave?

On the shore, dimly seen through the mists of the
  deep,
Where the foe's haughty host in dread silence
  reposes.

What is that which the breeze, o'er the towering
    steep,
As it fitfully blows, now conceals, now discloses?
Now it catches the gleam of the morning's first beam,
In full glory reflected now shines on the stream:
    'Tis the star-spangled banner! O long may it wave
    O'er the land of the free and the home of the
      brave!

And where is that band who so vauntingly swore
That the havoc of war and the battle's confusion
A home and a country should leave us no more?
Their blood has washed out their foul footsteps'
    pollution.
No refuge could save the hireling and slave
From the terror of flight, or the gloom of the grave:
    And the star-spangled banner in triumph doth
      wave
    O'er the land of the free and the home of the
      brave!

Oh! thus be it ever, when freemen shall stand
Between their loved homes and the war's desolation!
Blest with victory and peace, may the heaven-
    rescued land
Praise the Power that hath made and preserved us a
    nation.
Then conquer we must, for our cause it is just,
And this be our motto: "In God is our trust."
    And the star-spangled banner in triumph shall
      wave
    O'er the land of the free and the home of the
      brave!

CHAPTER ⋄ 8

Holidays in Your
New Culture

There is gladness in remembrance.

—Canadian proverb

Your parents no doubt preserve the ethnic celebrations associated with their country or culture. By this means you become familiar with festivals, ceremonies, and foods that mean so much to them. You will appreicate this familiarity more and more as the years go by.

Perhaps the holidays that are observed in the United States or in Canada are not so familiar to you. This chapter provides some information about days that mark special events of the past or honor persons who have made significant contributions to their country's progress.

The United States observes many holidays. The President and Congress can proclaim holidays for the District of Columbia and for federal employees. These are called federal holidays. The individual states have power to

legislate their own holidays. To illustrate, Vermont celebrates the Battle of Bennington because it was fought in that state (during the War of Independence), and Missouri celebrates the birthday of President Harry Truman, a native of that state. Most states also observe the federal holidays.

Don't expect mail delivery on these days, the federal holidays: New Year's Day, Martin Luther King, Jr. Day, Washington's Birthday, Memorial Day, Independence Day, Labor Day, Columbus Day, Veterans' Day, Thanksgiving Day, and Christmas. When a holiday falls on a Sunday or on a Saturday, it may be ruled that its observance take place on the Monday that follows or on the preceding Friday. This is intended to give people long weekends.

New Year's Day begins the calendar year. New Year's Eve, which is the evening of the last day of the old year, is a time for parties at which people wait for the new year to arrive at midnight. In bygone days many people went to church for a watch-night service. Some religious persons still do that. On New Year's Day football enthusiasts watch college bowl games on TV (Rose Bowl at Pasadena, Cotton Bowl at Dallas, Orange Bowl at Miami, etc.) and the lavish parades associated with them. In general, New Year's is a time for thinking about the past and contemplating the future. Traditionally, resolutions are made to do better than in the past. In illustrations, an old man represents the outgoing year and a newborn babe the incoming one.

Martin Luther King, Jr. Day honors the black Baptist minister and civil rights leader who was born in Georgia, became an eloquent and inspiring orator, and received

the Nobel Prize for Peace in 1964. Four years later he was assassinated by an escaped white convict. King was born on January 15, 1929, but the celebration of his birth is held on the Monday that follows January 15.

George Washington (1732–1799) is commonly known as the "father of his country." He became a surveyor, but soon sought a military career in the colonial forces of the British. (The United States had not yet gained independence.) After notable service in the French and Indian War, he returned to private life at Mount Vernon, the Virginia plantation he had inherited. Between 1759 and 1775 he served in his state's legislature and then briefly as a delegate to the Continental Congress, the federal legislature of the thirteen colonies. The Revolution—also known as the War of Independence—began, and in 1775 Washington became commander-in-chief-of the Continental Army. He faced serious difficulties such as lack of equipment, poor pay for his soldiers, short enlistment periods, and desertions. Nevertheless, in 1781 he succeeded, with the help of the French government, in forcing the British to surrender. When a government was formed according to the specifications of the newly written Constitution, Washington was unanimously chosen to be the nation's first President. He took office in 1789 and served two four-year terms, refusing a third. His birthday is February 22, but it is celebrated on the third Monday in February.

Memorial Day is sometimes called Decoration Day because it is a time to honor our war dead by placing flowers in cemeteries. Begun in 1868, it was originally meant for decoration of the graves of Civil War veterans. It is currently celebrated on the last Monday in May.

Independence Day, better known as the Fourth of July, commemorates the adoption of the Declaration of

Independence in 1776. That act created a country independent of England. John Adams, a signer of the Declaration and successor to Washington as President, wrote to his wife, Abigail, when the Declaration was adopted: "I am apt to believe that [the day] will be celebrated by succeeding generations as the great anniversary festival." He was correct. Celebrations include parades and fireworks. Many people celebrate by having family picnics or barbeques.

Labor Day was instituted in 1882 by the Knights of Labor to honor workers, and Congress made it a national holiday in 1894. In a way, it marks the end of summer— school generally opens the day after Labor Day.

Columbus Day commemorates the discovery of the American continent by Christopher Columbus on October 12, 1492. Columbus, a native of Genoa, Italy, sailing under Spanish auspices, went ashore on San Salvador Island in the Bahamas. He thought he had reached the East Indies by sailing west. After returning to Europe, he made three additional voyages to the New World and was largely responsible for the establishment of Spanish culture. Columbus Day, which is celebrated on a Monday, holds special significance for Italian-Americans.

Veterans' Day began as Armistice Day, which marked the end of World War I on November 11, 1918. It now honors veterans of all wars and is observed on a Monday.

Thanksgiving exemplifies the influence of the Pilgrims on the American culture. In 1621, William Bradford, who governed the Plymouth colony for many years, arranged a celebration that included Indians who had been friendly to the colonists. The preceding winter had been harsh. Of the 102 who had sailed in the *Mayflower* from England to

the New World, 47 had died. With the harvest now safely in, Bradford sought to thank God for His bounty. Four wild turkeys were shot and served at that first Thanksgiving feast. Today turkey is traditional at a Thanksgiving dinner, as are cranberries and pumpkin pie. George Washington was the first President to proclaim Thanksgiving a holiday. Since 1939 it has been celebrated on the fourth Thursday of November. At the present time many families reunite at Thanksgiving. They eat (and drink) too much and watch parades and football on TV. Christmas shoppers flock to malls and stores on the day after Thanksgiving, and merchants expect sales that day to be the best of the year.

Christmas is the great festival of the Christian world, a celebration of the birth of Jesus Christ in Bethlehem almost 2000 years ago. It is a time when Christians are reminded to show goodwill to their fellow men. Giving gifts is traditional and is symbolic of God's gift of His son to mankind. Friends exchange greeting cards, families decorate trees, mothers prepare favorite foods, and so on. Santa Claus is a mythical person who delivers presents in a sleigh drawn by reindeer. Christmas has become so commercialized that sometimes its fundamental significance is overlooked: It is a religious commemoration. There is growing resentment by non-Christians when the religious aspects of Christmas intrude into public matters. Many stories and poems have been written about Christmas; one of the most famous is *A Christmas Carol* by Charles Dickens. Christmas is always celebrated on December 25.

If you know even a little American history, you may be wondering why Lincoln's birthday, which is February 12, is not on the federal list. As the sixteenth President,

Abraham Lincoln (1809–1865) successfully led a nation divided over slavery through a devastating Civil War. He held the union of states together and was able to abolish slavery. Even today he is not popular in some of the states that fought on the side of the Confederacy (composed of the Southern states that temporarily left the Union), and that may account for the omission noted. However, many states now have a combination celebration, on a Monday, of Washington's and Lincoln's birthdays. It is called Presidents' Day.

Several other days that cannot be called holidays are regularly celebrated by large numbers of people.

Valentine's Day, February 14, is a time for sending greeting cards, often decorated with hearts, to loved ones. Some people associate the day with a St. Valentine, but most think it was originally connected to the Roman fertility festival of the Lupercalia, celebrated on February 15.

St. Patrick's Day, April 17, brings out the Irish, all wearing shamrocks. There are parades in many cities, the best known in New York and Boston. St. Patrick lived, but so much myth is associated with him that it is difficult to separate fact from fiction. Toward the end of his life, he wrote the *Confessions*, which was autobiographical in nature, and this has provided some reliable information. Born in England about 385, he was captured by Irish raiders in his youth. After working as a herdsman, he escaped from Ireland to continental Europe. After becoming a priest, he had a vision that his mission was to Christianize pagan, or heathen, Ireland. In this St. Patrick was successful, preserving some good aspects of Celtic culture and maintaining some of the humane aspects of Christianity.

Easter Sunday is known as a movable feast because it does not occur on the same date every year; it falls between March 22 and April 25. It commemorates Christ's resurrection from the dead, a very important event to Christians.

Mothers' Day and **Fathers' Day** fall on the second Sunday in May (since 1914, by Congressional resolution) and on the third Sunday in June (since 1971), respectively. These days honor parents. Carnations are associated with Mothers' Day.

Flag Day is celebrated on June 14. It was first requested in 1894 by the Sons of the Revolution and the Colonial Dames of America. Proclaimed in 1941, it observes the adoption by Congress of the first national flag (see p. 57).

Halloween occurs on October 31, the day before All Saints Day. Kids dress up in costumes and go from house to house begging for "treats." Black cats, pumpkins, ghosts, and witches all symbolize Halloween, a day when the ancients believed that evil spirits walked on the earth.

Election Day is not a celebration; nevertheless, it is extremely important. Every four years, on the Tuesday following the first Monday in November, the citizens of the United States elect a President. (Many other officials are elected at the same time.) The right to vote is to be prized. People who have lived in countries with governments ruled by force appreciate that fact.

The story that follows was written by the author for a magazine issue celebrating the Fourth of July.

Uncle Sam

On the Fourth of July, Uncle Sam represents us all and is regarded in a kindly light. Close to April 15, when

income tax reports are due, he is likely to undergo a temporary loss in popularity; he is no longer "we," but "they," meaning the government.

Customarily depicted as a cartoon figure with white hair and goatee, swallow-tailed coat, jacket decorated with stars, striped pants, and top hat with stars and stripes, he presents a patriotic figure.

There is considerable evidence that his original model was one Samuel Wilson of Troy, New York.

Wilson was born in 1766 in Massachusetts, one of thirteen children. Fourteen years later the family moved to New Hampshire. Samuel and his brother Ebenezer eventually found their way on foot to Troy, where they did bricklaying. The year 1793 saw them start a meat-packing business that was to prove successful. By the time the War of 1812 broke out, Samuel, approaching middle age, was known to many in his community as Uncle Sam.

The war brought him a contract to supply the Army with beef and pork, and it was his habit to stamp on each barrel the letters U.S., which at the time were not commonly used as initials for United States. The story goes that when the governor of New York inquired what the letters stood for, he was jokingly told they meant Uncle Sam.

Wilson lived for almost 88 years, dying in 1854. A short time after his death, the Albany *Evening Journal* wrote that the letters "were at first taken to be initials of 'Uncle Sam' Wilson, but finally lost their local significance and became, throughout the Army, the familiar term for 'United States.'" This seems to confirm the impression that Uncle Sam and the U.S. had become synonymous.

It is not clear how the artistic representation of the character evolved. We do know that in 1851 a man calling

Recruiting poster (courtesy Library of Congress).

himself Uncle Sam appeared in a parade at Amesbury, Massachusetts.

In 1916 illustrator James Montgomery Flagg, while commissioned by the State of New York as a military

artist, painted the Uncle Sam shown here. The War Department added the words I WANT YOU, producing a very effective recruiting poster—so effective in World War I that it was revived and used again in World War II.

Norman Rockwell, America's best-loved artist, gave Uncle Sam wings in a 1928 *Saturday Evening Post* cover drawing promoting aviation.

The year 1962 brought a national observance of the sesquicentennial of the birth of the Uncle Sam story. In the previous year a resolution of Congress had recognized "Uncle" Samuel Wilson as the namesake of the tall man with the goatee.

By the 1950s the State Department was seeking a new type of portrait—something not stern, but friendly and nonthreatening, suitable for embassies and consulates around the world. A sketch by the New York advertising artist Herbert Noxon proved appealing because the smiling subject was ready to shake hands, his facial expression "benign and not sharp and calculating . . ." On that basis, Noxon was commissioned to make an official portrait of Uncle Sam.

According to American historian Arthur Schlesinger, Jr., "Every generation recreates Uncle Sam in its own image." We cannot forecast the depictions to come, but it's a safe bet that on future Fourths of July, Uncle Sam's attire will still sport Old Glory.

Canada is less liberal than the United States in legalizing holidays. **New Year's Day** and **Christmas** fall on the same days as in the United States. **Easter Monday**, the day following Easter Sunday, is observed, as is **Boxing Day**, December 26. The latter holiday was begun in England, when boxed gifts were given to servants and tradesmen.

The Queen's Birthday is sometimes called Victoria Day. It honors Queen Victoria, who reigned over the British Empire from 1837 to 1901. Although she had little power, for England is a democracy, she had principles that commanded respect. Her name appeared throughout Canada; the city of Victoria was named for her, as was the Victorian Order of Nurses. She was born on May 24, 1801, but the holiday is now held on a Monday.

Canada Day, July 1, commemorates the beginning of Confederation in 1867. It is somewhat comparable to Independence Day in the United States.

Thanksgiving Day was adopted as a national holiday in 1879. It is now celebrated on the second Monday in October.

Remembrance Day, November 11, is the equivalent of Veterans' Day in the United States.

If you hold to the customs of your parents and also adopt those of the country to which you have immigrated, you will have taken an important step in biculturism.

CHAPTER 9

American as Apple Pie

Reality never surpasses imagination.
                                   —Canadian proverb

H ere we introduce two men whose works are part of American culture and should become familiar to you. Both men are now dead, but what they left continues to delight Americans of all ages.

The first story is about an artist. It was written by the author for a magazine.

Telling Stories with a Brush

Critics have called him a fine artist, a folk artist, and no artist at all; to the ordinary citizen Norman Rockwell is the best-known and best-loved American artist. During his unique career he designed humorous and serious magazine covers, advertisements, calendars, greeting cards, commemorative stamps; he illustrated such classics as *Tom Sawyer*; he painted the great and near-great;

he depicted social problems, and he gave this country inspirational works.

Rockwell was born in 1894 in New York City. His father managed a textile firm and as a hobby often copied magazine illustrations. Young Norman sometimes copied also, sometimes drew according to his imagination; he remembered producing his own version of Mr. Micawber while the senior Rockwell read from *David Copperfield*. The fact that her own father was an unsuccessful painter had embittered Rockwell's mother, and she did little to encourage her son to take up that profession.

But by age twelve Norman's aim in life was just that. He dropped out of high school to attend art school. At sixteen he was studying at the Art Students League, where he was influenced by the work of Howard Pyle, the famous illustrator noted for historical accuracy. There Rockwell worked hard learning basics. He was also impressed by a teacher named Thomas Fogarty, who defined illustration as an author's words in paint.

Rockwell became established professionally while still unusually young. At sixteen he was commissioned to design four Christmas cards for a rich woman; at seventeen he illustrated *Tell Me Why Stories*; at nineteen he was art director of *Boys' Life*; at twenty-two he did his first cover for the *Saturday Evening Post*. He was to do more than 300 covers for that publication; in fact, his name was synomynous with that of the *Post* until his tenure there ended in 1963.

Enlistment in the Navy during World War I took Rockwell to the Navy Yard at Charleston, South Carolina, where he was officially a third-class varnisher and painter. But the commanding officer allowed him to continue contributing to the *Post* and also assigned him to do portraits of visiting dignitaries.

During the 1920s Rockwell's work continued to improve. His financial success made it possible for him to study modern art in Paris. (He soon learned that abstract art was not his forte and decided to stick to what had been successful for him.) He had married Irene O'Connor at twenty-two, but she divorced him eleven years later.

Mary Barstow, a teacher, was Rockwell's second wife and the mother of his three sons. The marriage was a happy one, lasting from 1930 until 1959, when Mary died. During this period, Rockwell received numerous commissions and produced some of his best work. Never a city lover, he moved to Arlington, Vermont, in 1939 and remained there until 1953, when the family moved again—this time to Stockbridge, Massachusetts.

How did Rockwell go about producing a painting? After some years, he used this procedure. He first sketched his idea. Next he assembled models, costumes, background, and props and photographed them. Then he made a very detailed full-scale drawing, followed by a color sketch. The final step was a painting. He suffered from periods of self-doubt, and he was always a perfectionist, working extraordinarily hard to produce what satisfied him.

His work was noted for its authenticity, and he would go to great lengths to attain it. For a train scene, he once asked the Rutland Railway to leave a car side-tracked in Rutland, Vermont; in planning illustrations for *Huckleberry Finn*, he visited Hannibal, Missouri, the boyhood home of Mark Twain; in *Outside the Principal's Office*, he used a genuine black eye of a local boy, painting it over the undamaged skin of the girl.

The models deserve special mention. From the beginning, he selected them with care. However, he knew almost everyone in Arlington and later Stockbridge, and using neighbors and friends made his task easier. He was

noted for paying well, and most were flattered at being used. Eventually he assembled a collection of hundreds of costumes for these people. The model for Willie Gillis, World War II GI, was a Bob Buck, exempt from the draft, and thus suitable to use in a series. When Buck enlisted as a naval aviator, Rockwell cleverly created six generations of fighting Gillises, using head shots taken before Buck was sent to the Pacific. With Buck's return to civilian life, Willie Gillis attended college, as did real-life GIs. Susan E. Meyer's 1981 book, *Norman Rockwell's People*, has much information about the models.

Rockwell's creativity is obvious in his presentation of a scene: The viewer grasps the situation at a glance. Then in the way good writing evokes an emotional reponse, the painting causes laughter or empathy or some strong feeling. The feeling may be intensified by an expression on the face of the subject or just by the presence of a mutt in the picture.

In 1941, President Franklin D. Roosevelt mentioned the Four Freedoms—Freedom of Speech, Freedom of Worship, Freedom from Want, and Freedom from Fear—in an address to Congress. Rockwell depicted those freedoms in four paintings, but he could not persuade the government to use them as part of the war effort. In 1943, however, the *Post* ran them. They were later exhibited in sixteen leading cities and viewed by some million and a half people, and they helped to sell $133 million in government bonds. According to Ben Hibb, then editor of the *Post*, "To me [*The Four Freedoms*] are great human documents in the form of paint and canvas. A great picture, I think, is one which moves and inspires millions of people. *The Four Freedoms* did—and do."

After Mary's death, Rockwell married Molly Punderson, a retired school teacher. They traveled to such places as

India so he could paint Nehru, Cape Canaveral for the launching of astronauts, and Ethiopia to see the Peace Corps in action. Before he died in 1978, Rockwell had chronicled on canvas many of the major attitudes, events, and problems spanning half a century.

In answer to criticism that he failed to depict the seamy side of life, he contended that he painted life as he would like it to be. "If there were problems, there were humorous problems," he said.

His response to those who considered him no artist at all was: "I guess I am a storyteller and although this may not be the highest form of art, it is what I love to do."

Today the chief repositories of Rockwell originals are the Stockbridge Historical Society's Old Corner House and the Norman Rockwell Museum in Philadelphia. Throughout the country, copies are displayed as prints, and they appear on thousands of mugs, plates, and so on. Apparently Americans like a storyteller.

The second story is about a writer who was also a very successful artist.

His Naughty Cats Wear Hats

"He makes house calls in the land of our first dreams and fears, where naughty cats wear hats, and the menace of the Grinch is real."
— Citation, Doctor of Fine Arts
Princeton University, 1985

The Congressional Record of March 2, 1984, notes an unusual speech by Senator Patrick Daniel Moynihan:

Mr. President, Mr. President,
I rise to set a precedent.
With glee and with joy,
Like a five-year-old boy,
I rise to relate
Some news which is great.

The news was that Dr. Seuss—author and educator, advertising man, documentary filmmaker, political cartoonist, and illustrator—was that day celebrating his eightieth birthday.

The son of a baker's daughter and a German brewer (who later became zookeeper and parks superintendent), he was born Theodor Seuss Geisel in Springfield, Massachusetts, on March 2, 1904. Following graduation from Dartmouth College, he aspired to earn a Ph.D. in English literature. After brief contacts with curricula offered at Oxford and the Sorbonne, however, he abandoned the idea.

Although he lacked formal training in art, during his Dartmouth years he had done illustrations for the college's humor publication *Jack O'Lantern*. So it was not surprising that the year 1927 saw Geisel back in the United States working first as a free-lance cartoonist and beginning a career as an advertising artist.

For *Judge* magazine he drew a cartoon showing a medieval castle, an armored knight, and a dragon. In the caption, the medieval tenant exclaimed, "Darn it all, another dragon. And just after I'd sprayed the whole castle with Flit!" When the wife of a Standard Oil executive saw the cartoon, she persuaded her husband to hire Geisel as an advertising artist. (Standard Oil manufactured Flit, an insecticide.) Later he advertised Schaeffer Bock Beer, Ford Motor Company, Atlas Products, NBC

Radio, and other companies, but the "Quick, Henry! The Flit!" series was his most successful campaign. In 1927, deciding that his financial future was bright, he married Helen Palmer, whom he had met at Oxford. They remained happily married until she died forty years later.

In 1931 Geisel illustrated *Boners*, a collection of bloopers made by schoolchildren. ("A chiropodist is a man who trains birds to sing." is one of the definitions that he portrayed.) Apparently that experience prompted the idea of creating books for children. Then when crossing the Atlantic by ship in 1936, he scribbled some nonsensical thoughts to the rhythm of the engines: "A stupid horse and wagon . . . horse and chariot . . . chariot pulled by flying cat . . . flying cat pulling at Viking ship . . . And this is a story that no one can beat . . . I saw it all happen on Mulberry Street." The final result was a story about a boy whose imagination transforms Mulberry Street into a wondrous place. *And to Think That I Saw It on Mulberry Street* was so different from the children's books then on the market that twenty-eight publishing houses rejected it before Vanguard Press put it out. The author called himself Dr. Seuss, explaining later, "The 'Dr. Seuss' is a combination of my middle name and the fact that I had been studying for my doctorate when I quit to become a cartoonist. My father had always wanted to see a Dr. in front of my name, so I attached it."

Next came *The 500 Hats of Bartholomew Cubbins*, followed by many self-illustrated juveniles that firmly established Dr. Seuss as a favorite children's writer, noted for imaginative plots and characters described in witty and often nonsensical verses accompanied by unique drawings.

From 1943 to 1946 he served in the Informational and Educational Division of the Army Signal Corps. Sent to

Hollywood, he learned animation. During this time he wrote and produced a two-reel film, *Your Job in Germany*, which won a 1945 Academy Award.

Author John Hersey in 1954 wrote an essay in *Life* about the problems young children encounter when they start to read. Geisel changed the situation with *The Cat in the Hat*, which uses only 223 different words, all words that a youngster can master. At the same time, the child's interest is whetted and sustained. In this book, the reader encounters a bored Sally and her brother on a rainy day. But they are not bored for long . . .

> We looked!
> And we saw him!
> The Cat in the Hat!

With flair the brash, confident cat makes an entrance, umbrella in hand. With Thing One and Thing Two from his hat he soon causes incredible havoc. Then just when the children's mother is about to return, the cat suddenly produces his picker-upper that marvelously restores order.

> Then he said, "That is that."
> And he was gone
> With a tip of his hat.

But to the delight of multitudes of children, he returns in *The Cat in the Hat Comes Back*. The first cat book was so well received that the publisher, Random House, created a special division named Beginner Books, with Seuss as president.

Seuss encouraged other aspects of his readers' learning; for example, *The Lorax* is about environmental pollution, and *The Butter Battle Book* deals with the nuclear arms

race. He followed the examples of Grimm and Andersen in never talking down to his young audience. He also realized that children have a strong ethical sense and "want to see virtue rewarded and arrogance or meanness punished." So while he entranced their little minds with the cat's outrageous antics that must bring them vicarious pleasure, he also demonstrated the cat's sense of responsibility by inventing for him a magical picker-upper to clean up the mess. Geisel was a perfectionist who spent much time and effort on his productions.

He is the author of a novel written when he was twenty-two. It was, according to him, "very long and mercifully never published." An older Dr. Seuss remarked, "I picked up the manuscript a few years ago— and couldn't understand a word of it."

Seuss has written adult books such as *The Seven Lady Godivas* and *You're Only Old Once!*; movie and filmstrip adaptations have been made of many of his works and TV animated specials, notably of *The Grinch Who Stole Christmas*, *Horton Hears a Who*, and *The Lorax*. He had no children of his own, but millions of children have read his books, which have been translated into some twenty languages. He was the recipient of Oscars, Emmys, and other awards as well as of honorary degrees.

For many years he lived in a mountaintop house in La Jolla, California, with his second wife, Audrey Stone Diamond, whom he married in 1968. The home contains his studio, which overlooks the Pacific. Despite cataracts, a heart attack, and cancer operations, he had the satisfaction of seeing his *Oh, the Places You'll Go!* published in 1990. He died in 1991.

The nation's debt to Theodor Seuss Geisel is well expressed in the citation of his 1984 Pulitzer Prize. It notes his "special contribution for nearly half a century to the

education and enjoyment of America's children and their parents."

If you don't recognize Rockwell prints, you will in time, because they can be seen in so many different places. If you have brothers or sisters or nephews or nieces too young to read by themselves, try a Dr. Seuss book on them. You will enjoy it as much as they.

CHAPTER ◇ 10

European Immigrants— The Golden Door

... few immigrants can be induced to sail for any other destination.

—*New York Times*, 1874

C ountries like Japan have few immigrants. For that reason, there is little mix of nationalities and races, and the Japanese people are called homogeneous. The United States and Canada, in contrast, have a mosaic population, composed of various races from many nations.

Europe was once the homeland of most immigrants who came to America. Not all spoke English, but almost all belonged to the Caucasian (white) race. Because that culture still dominates America, it is important for you to understand how it persisted.

The United States began its existence as an independent nation in 1776. Although it was not until 1820 that immigration records were kept, much is known about the people who lived during the Revolution and the period that followed. According to the first Census, which was taken in 1790, the total population was slightly less than four million. For comparison, this is only a few more than the number of people in the city of Los Angeles today. Most lived along the Atlantic coast, where Philadelphia was the largest and most prosperous city. The port cities of Boston, New York, Baltimore, and Charleston had become the centers of commerce. The Appalachian Mountains constituted the western frontier, beyond which lay a vast and unsettled region.

About half of the people were of English descent, with many of them settled in New England. When the Revolution began, about 80,000 of them, known as United Empire Loyalists, left the colonies for Canada to avoid taking up arms against the motherland. (Canada's population was so small that the presence of this relatively large number of newcomers strengthened English influence in a country of French origin.) The newly formed United States also had representatives of other nationalities: for example, Dutch in New York; Danes, Finns, and Swedes in the Delaware Valley; Germans in some areas of Pennsylvania and the Southern states; and Scottish-Irish in the rugged mountains of the frontier of the South.

Afro-Americans accounted for about one fifth of the population. They or their forebears had been forcibly brought to North America from Africa. Most were slaves on Southern plantations. Importing slaves to the United States became illegal in 1808. Nevertheless, slave traders

managed to smuggle in 1,000 slaves a year up to the time of the Civil War.

Why had these early immigrants made a hazardous journey by sailing ship to a land so far from home? Thomas Paine, author of some of the greatest political pamphlets of all time, cited the most important reason when he called the United States an "asylum for the persecuted lovers of civil and religious liberty from every part of Europe." Before the War of Independence, some of the immigrants were convicts who were deported from England. Often their offenses were what we would consider minor today. (After 1776 such convicts were sent to Australia because the United States no longer permitted England to "dump" its criminals in the new nation.) Then, as always, there were immigrants who came in search of the adventure the New World offered.

Almost half of the early immigrants were indentured servants. The word *indenture* means contract. An indentured servant was bound by contract to work for a specified time—usually four years—for the person who had paid for the immigrant's passage. These indentured people would not be free until they had served the required time, but the prospect of ultimate freedom made them different from the black slaves. (In time, contract labor was outlawed.)

The immigrants to colonial America represented many walks of life, though the majority of them came from humble backgrounds. The class barriers they had known in Europe no longer existed. Also, the ease of acquiring land enabled them to improve their lot, provided they were willing to work hard.

What happened to the Native Americans—the original Americans? By 1800 white settlers had driven some tribes

into the Appalachian Mountains and beyond. As westward expansion continued, the Indians were subjected to much inhumane treatment.

Historians agree that during its first fifty years the United States received only a trickle of immigrants. One reason was that Europe was occupied with the Napoleonic Wars from 1803 until 1815.

But the American population was augmented from another source. In 1803, for the sum of $15 million, the nation acquired from France millions of acres of land. Called the Louisiana Purchase, the area extended roughly from the Mississippi River to the Rocky Mountains and from the Gulf of Mexico to British North America. It was populated by 200,000 Spanish, French, and Indians, to whom Uncle Sam granted citizenship and religious freedom. (Still more land was obtained from Spain after the Mexican War.)

Now that the western frontier was closer to the Pacific Ocean than to the Mississippi River, it was evident that the nation lacked sufficient manpower to clear, cultivate, and defend the land, to homestead, to build roads, and to carry on the many tasks necessary in a society that was becoming more industrialized. Until well into the 20th century, Europe continued to supply much of this.

Emigration from that continent increased dramatically between 1820 and 1860. Population growth, lack of land suitable for cultivation, crop failure, and the effects of the Industrial Revolution all contributed. The French Revolution had given many common people expectations that were not being met at home, and America with all its land and industry seemed very attractive.

The first iron-hulled steamship crossed the Atlantic Ocean in 1843. Although the sailing ship remained in vogue for many years longer, its demise was on the way.

As the time required for the voyage shortened and the cost fell, steamship companies vigorously promoted immigration to America. Letters from earlier immigrants to relatives at home were also influential; most of them portrayed the New World as the land of opportunity, downplaying any negatives.

In the years between 1840 and 1860 the largest number of immigrants came from Ireland. Between 1845 and 1849 Irish potatoes were infected with a fungus that destroyed them. This was especially serious because potatoes were the mainstay of the diet of the poor. A million persons died during those years, and by 1860 another million and a half Irishmen had fled to the United States.

During the same period, 1840–1860, Germany furnished the second-largest number of European immigrants, followed by England, France, Scotland, Scandinavia, Switzerland, Belgium, and the Netherlands.

Immigration from the Far East began in 1849 when gold was discovered in California. People from many parts of the world rushed to the area to make quick fortunes; in three years California's population increased 25 times. By 1852 it included 25,000 Chinese. Signs of discrimination against them soon became evident: They were driven from their claims by white prospectors, and there was even objection to their working near mining camps. The governor of California termed them "incapable of being assimilated and dangerous to the welfare of the state."

American citizenship was easily obtained in the 1860s. The immigrant reported his arrival at a court of record and received a dated certificate. Following five years of residence in the country, a certificate of naturalization was issued, conferring the right to vote and even to run for political office.

By the 1820s the frontier had advanced to the Mississippi

and Missouri Rivers. By the 1840s pioneers had crossed the Great Plains into the Utah, California, and Oregon territories.

Most Native American tribes could not prevent this inexorable expansion. They were blocked by the military, while the slaughter of the buffalo and the introduction of smallpox, tuberculosis, venereal disease, and whiskey by the white man contributed to their weakness. By the outbreak of the Civil War, only the Plains Indians were able to obstruct this westward push. And that was a temporary diversion.

As the 1860s began, "American fever"—the urge to immigrate to the United States—had increased the nation's population to 31 million.

During the tragic Civil War, both Union and Confederate forces attracted foreign-born volunteers. Most fought for the North, and according to historian Bruce Catton, the experience somehow Americanized them.

One immigrant group deserves special mention because it is so unusual. Between 1880 and 1890 more than half of the Irish immigrants were women—most of them single and under thirty-five. They worked as live-in servants of one type or another, saving their earnings usually for the church or to pay passage for relatives to come to America. It was not long, however, before these newcomers sought upward mobility; and they were successful in nursing, teaching, and other professions.

The Superintendent of the Census declared in 1880 that the United States no longer had a frontier. Although millions of acres were still available for homesteading, most of the land was too arid to be useful. Large areas of the country were now industrialized, but Idaho, North Dakota, Oklahoma, Mississippi, and Arkansas remained more than 90 percent rural.

There was in the 67th New York Infantry a young German named Sebastian Muller, who got off an immigrant ship in 1860 and walked the streets unable to find work because he could speak no English and because times in this land of promise were harder than he had supposed they would be. The war came and in 1861 a recruiting agent got him, and to his people back in the fatherland Muller wrote: "I am a volunteer soldier in the Army of the United States, to fight the rebels of South America for a sacred thing. All of America has to become free and united and the starry banner has to fly again over the new world. Then we also want to have the slaves freed, the trading of human beings must have an end and every slave should be set free and on his own in time. . . . Evil of all kinds, thievery, whoring, lying and deception have to be punished here."

Muller served in the 67th and on June 20, 1864, the regiment's time expired and it was sent back for muster-out. But he had enlisted a couple of months late, and he and a few others were held in service and were transferred to the 65th New York to serve out their time, and two days after the 67th went back home Muller was a picket in an advanced gun pit on the VI Corps front, and a Rebel sniper drew a bead on him and killed him. A German comrade wrote a letter of consolation to Muller's parents: "If a person is meant to die on land, he will not drown. If death on the battlefield is to be his lot, he will not die in the cradle. God's dispositions are wise and his ways are inscrutable." The chaplain added a note saying that Muller had died without pain and had been given "a decent Christian burial." That was that.

In the 19th Massachusetts there was an Irish sergeant named Mike Scannell—[who had] won his chevrons by carrying the flag at Cold Harbor—and in the II Corps debacle over by the Jerusalem Plank Road Mike and his flag were out in front and were taken by the Confederates, one of whom came at Mike with leveled bayonet, ordering: "You damned Yankee, give me that flag!" Mike looked at the Southerner and he looked at the bayonet, and he replied:

"Well, it is twenty years since I came to his country, and you are the first man who ever called me a Yankee. You can take the flag, for that compliment."

Nothing much had happened. A German who could not tell Virginia from South America had seen a sacred thing in the war and had died for it, and an Irishman after twenty years of rejection had been accepted, at the point of a bayonet but in the language of his time and place, as a full-fledged American.

The synthesis was taking place.

In *A Stillness at Appomattox,* historian Bruce Catton illustrates how the Civil War Americanized two immigrants.

Many opportunities were open to immigrants as the country approached the twentieth century. The steel industry, for example, was directly and indirectly responsible for significant employment. Iron ore deposits were discovered in Minnesota in 1887. The ore was shoveled into railroad cars bound for Duluth. From there it was transported by Great Lakes steamers to Chicago, where it was shipped to steel refineries in various locations. The entire process provided numerous jobs for unskilled labor—in mines and mills and on trains, docks, and ships. Unlike the situation today, most of the immigrants were unskilled.

New York was the chief point of entry when immigrants arrived by ship. Even now, when foreigners from Europe are not numerous and when air travel has supplanted ocean travel, the Big Apple remains a major port of entry.

Intertwined with the history of immigration to the United States is the story of the Statue of Liberty. Lady Liberty, situated on Liberty (formerly Bedloe's) Island, is not an American creation. She is a gift of the people of France to the people of the United States to commemorate "the alliance of the two nations in achieving the independence of the United States of America."

The recipient country had agreed to provide a pedestal for the statue, but private donations came in very slowly. A literary woman named Emma Lazarus was asked to write an appropriate poem that could be auctioned off, the proceeds to be used to bolster the pedestal fund. Miss Lazarus, whose roots were Jewish, was well acquainted with many immigrants who in the early 1880s had fled Russian pogroms, organized massacres of helpless people.

With such unfortunate victims in mind, she composed "The New Colossus." Its sale did add to the pedestal fund, but the poem had significance for a different reason.

Emma Lazarus (courtesy Library of Congress).

As you read the sonnet, you will see why it eventually gave a special meaning to the huge and imposing statue first seen by newcomers as their ship sailed into New York harbor. Irving Berlin, himself an immigrant from

Russia, set "The New Colossus" to haunting music, and the last five lines are familiar to millions of American citizens.

For newcomers who now arrive by air in Los Angeles, for example, Lady Liberty may not be important. However, many European immigrants who arrived years ago feel so strongly now that they request that their ashes be scattered over the Statue of Liberty.

Between 1855 and 1890 an offshore receiving center called Castle Garden processed about eight million people entering New York City from Europe. After Castle Garden was destroyed by fire, an immigrant depot center was constructed on Ellis Island. The first entrant came in 1892 and the last in 1954. A restored Ellis Island is now part of the Statue of Liberty National Monument.

Pages and pages have been written about the immigrants' fear of failing to get through Ellis Island. They knew that the law barred persons with physical deformities, mental deficiencies, and the like, because such persons might have to be cared for at public expense. There were other reasons for deportation, and the newcomers worried about giving unacceptable answers to the many questions they would be asked.

Lined up in groups of thirty, they were rushed along, made to carry all their possessions with them. The medical examination was particularly dreaded because certain conditions meant detention or deportation. Temporary separation—for instance, when a sick child was taken from its mother to the contagion wards—might terrorize one or both. When one member of a family faced deportation, the others were in turmoil; a child under ten had to be accompanied by a close relative; if an adult were rejected, how would the children manage? And so it went. Actually, no more than two percent of the total

THE NEW COLOSSUS

Not like the brazen giant of Greek fame,
With conquering limbs astride from land to land,
Here at our sea-washed, sunset gates shall stand
A mighty woman with a torch, whose flame
Is the imprisoned lightning, and her name
Mother of Exiles. From her beacon-hand
Glows world-wide welcome; her mild eyes command
The air-bridged harbor that twin cities frame.

"Keep, ancient lands, your storied pomp!" cries she
With silent lips. "Give me your tired, your poor,
Your huddled masses yearning to breathe free,
The wretched refuse of your teeming shore,
Send these, the homeless, tempest-tossed to me:
I lift my lamp beside the golden door."

—Emma Lazarus
1883

immigrants in one year were deported. But faced with deportation, it was not unusual for the immigrant to commit suicide. That tells us something about the life he sought to change.

From the many accounts available, the officials in charge appear for the most part to have been insensitive to the situation. There is no doubt that they were pressed for time, and there was always a shortage of interpreters, which undoubtedly caused misunderstandings and unnecessary worry. There are documented reports of how foreign names were changed forever at Ellis Island, some through ignorance, some through misunderstanding, and some through arrogance on the part of officials.

Landing at Ellis Island, 1902 (courtesy Library of Congress).

Once the processing had been completed satisfactorily, a woman often waited to be met by a spouse or a relative not seen for years—or even by a stranger about to marry her because of an arrangement made by her family. All men and women who were not rejected boarded a ferry for Manhattan and a new life.

For the hordes that settled in the slums, life was far from easy. The conditions in 1890 are described in *How the Other Half Lives* by Danish immigrant Jacob Riis. He explained how the newcomer had to contend with unbelievable overcrowding in airless, firetrap tenements, with deplorable sanitation, with filth, disease, and crime in a strange environment where even drinking water was scarce in murderous summer heat.

The skills that had been valuable in agriculture were not needed in the city, so most of the immigrants were forced to take unskilled jobs at low wages, often in sweatshops. Those who did not understand English were especially at a disadvantage. Since ethnic groups tended to remain together, there was little opportunity for improving English.

The 1900 Census recorded 76 million people living in the United States. Roughly 88 percent were descended from white Europeans, and 12 percent of black African stock. The Native Americans numbered only 237,000. There were about 115,000 Orientals.

The Spanish-American War of 1898 had left the United States with complete ownership of Puerto Rico and Guam in addition to the Philippine Islands. Hawaii was annexed, and Uncle Sam had also formally occupied Wake Island. These new acquisitions meant that nine million people were living under the Stars and Stripes in outlying territories; few of them, however, were granted citizenship.

The United States had become the leader of the in-

Irving Berlin. Born in Russia, Berlin was brought to New York when he was four years old. His rabbi father was fleeing religious persecution. Berlin composed the music and lyrics for numerous popular musicals. He wrote "God Bless America" as an "expression of my gratitude to the country that inspired it" (courtesy Library of Congress).

dustrialized world. Of the immigrants seeking its benefits, most were now from southern Italy. The ranks were also swelled by Slavs—Poles, Czechs, Croats—and by refugees from Tsarist Russia. After 1900 increased numbers of Japanese began to arrive. More than one million immigrants were admitted in the years 1905, 1906, 1910, 1913, and 1914. The peak year was 1907, when 1.3 million arrived.

This was the era of the settlement house, established in poor areas of cities to aid the neighboring community. Hull House in Chicago was one of the most famous. Most settlement workers believed firmly in teaching immigrants to adopt American ways as rapidly as possible. They wished to make one out of many. A 1908 play, *The Melting Pot*, gave a name to this doctrine, which was in vogue for about half a century. The mosaic concept is currently in favor.

Present Theodore Roosevelt had said that when a person is loyal to the United States, national origin makes no difference, for that person "is just as good an American as anyone else."

World War I proved him correct when Americans of all origins served their adopted country in various ways. During that conflict the Russian Revolution of 1917 caused unwarranted fears that radicals might in some way cause peril to the government. A radical is a person who favors rapid and drastic changes in laws and methods of government. Immigrants, especially the "different" ones, were often considered radicals, and efforts were made to limit the entrance of such.

In the 1920s immigration was slowed by the passage of restrictive laws. Later the Great Depression proved a serious deterrent. This widespread economic slump began in 1929 and lasted for ten years. By 1932 roughly one of every four employable persons was out of work. Almost

Greta Garbo. Garbo came to the United States from Sweden. According to one authority, she is "perhaps the most celebrated motion-picture actress of all time, a provocative enignatic embodiment of feminine beauty and mystery" (courtesy Library of Congress).

every family in the country was affected. When jobs were plentiful and foreigners were needed to fill them, immigration was encouraged. Now the situation had changed, and aliens were not wanted.

Many foreigners were so discouraged that they returned home. In the early 1930s more people were leaving than entering the country. During the 1920s Mexicans had begun to arrive. As the Depression worsened, a great many crossed the Rio Grande again because there was nothing for them in the United States.

Adolf Hitler assumed power in Germany in 1934. As his persecution of Jews mounted, many of them sought refuge in the United States. Some 250,000 refugees did enter under the quota or were exempted as scholars. Countless others fleeing for their lives were refused entry, largely because of pressure from unions. It is particularly unfortunate that in 1939 some 20,000 German children, most of them Jewish, were refused.

That same year saw the start of World War II. Since then the European immigrants have declined in numbers, and consequently their influence is beginning to wane.

But they cannot be overlooked; multitudes of them arrived, suffered, and sacrificed. They remained ambitious for their children, believing that they themselves were also far better off than if they had remained in the Old Country. Their children attended public schools, learned English, and rapidly became Americanized. Countless first- and second-generation immigrants—Jews in particular— took advantage of the educational opportunities of New York City. All these immigrants have made marks in about every field of human endeavor, great and small. Their influence extends to numerous facets of our lives today, and their accomplishments will give you pride in carrying on their tradition.

CHAPTER 11

Canada—The True North Strong and Free*

A policy of multiculturism within a bilingual framework commends itself to the government as the most suitable means of assuring the cultural freedom of Canadians. . . .
—Prime Minister Pierre Elliott Trudeau, 1971

Today Canada and the United States have in common their European heritage and the English language as well as similar economic systems and political philosophies. Although their governments have different structures, both are democracies. Since 1982, Great Britain has had no control over the Canadian government. Note the key word "free" in the titles of this chapter and Chapter 14.

---

* From "O Canada" by Robert Stanley Weir (1856–1926).

Critics of the United States and Canada may question whether there is justice for all, but they seldom complain about freedom.

For many years immigration from Canada to the United States was frequent, both for native- and foreign-born Canadians. When better economic conditions below the border beckoned, many left Canada. Since 1965 this has not been a major problem.

Both countries have pluses and minuses. For instance, Canada's socialized medicine is much admired, and maintaining law and order is much less a problem there than in the United States. On the other hand, the type of deep-rooted antagonism that exists between English and French Canadians does not plague the United States.

The world associates Canada with champion hockey players, with historic Quebec and its French customs, with the magnificent Parliament buildings in Ottawa, with mineral wealth, wheat-producing prairies, great forests, mounted police, Canadian Brass, losses at Dieppe in World War II, the discovery of insulin—and more. The names of individuals come to mind—singer Anne Murray, actor Raymond Massey, photographer Yousuf Karsh (who emigrated from Armenia), poet Robert Service, humorist Stephen Leacock, author Lucy Maude Montgomery—and the list goes on and on. Little is known about the history of the country. This chapter will give you an overview of how Canada developed into the great nation that it is today.

The original inhabitants were Indians and Eskimos. The latter are now called Inuit. It is believed that Viking adventurers visited at the end of the tenth century but did not form permanent communities.

The first white people to colonize Canada were the French. They developed a fur trade with the Indians and

by 1608 had built a wooden fort and trading post at what is now Quebec City.

The English challenged French rule. They regarded as legitimate John Cabot's 1497 discovery of the east coast of Canada and his claim of it in the name of the King of England. They considered the French usurpers. In 1689, England and France were at war in Europe, and for almost three quarters of a century the two countries clashed in North America. (The series of conflicts are known to many as the French and Indian Wars.) Quebec fell to the English in 1759, and four years later the Treaty of Paris established English domination. France ceded all of its New World possessions to England except for the Louisiana Territory, which went to Spain. (Later this was transferred to France.)

Through the Quebec Act of 1774 the French retained the rights to their own language, religion, and civil law. In short, the groundwork was laid for a bicultural society; today both English and French are the official languages of the Canadian government (and of the province of New Brunswick). French is the official language of the province of Quebec and is used throughout Canada.

English settlements had been established in Newfoundland in 1610 and in Nova Scotia in 1629, and the founding of more continued. In 1670, Charles II granted to the Hudson's Bay Company monopoly trading rights over Rupert's Land, a huge unmapped area surrounding Hudson Bay. This company did much to increase settlement and English influence by establishing outposts in the wilderness. (Modern Winnipeg is close to the company's old Red River post.) The Hudson's Bay Company wanted furs from trappers. When men's beaver hats were fashionable in Europe, the animal most prized was the beaver. Compared to the thirteen colonies to the south, the

northern region was far less populous and less developed, much of it icebound for many months of the year and much of it almost uninhabitable.

Nevertheless, exploration took place. There had been fruitless attempts for years to discover a northwest passage to Asia out of Hudson Bay. By 1771 it was realized that no such passage existed, but the search for it was behind much exploration of the vast territory west of the bay. Not until 1800 was the shape of the continent of North America clearly known, and even then the details of much of the interior were obscure.

The Canadian colonies did not participate in. the War of Independence; they remained a group of English colonies. As we have seen, they became home to the United Empire Loyalists who left the thirteen rebellious colonies.

The Constitutional Act of 1791 divided the old inland French colony into Upper and Lower Canada, corresponding to today's Ontario and Quebec provinces. The latter remained predominantly French-speaking; the former became predominantly English-speaking as settlers from Scotland and from both Catholic and Protestant Ireland poured in during the 1800s.

The Civil War in the United States exerted an interesting effect on Canada's progress. It emphasized the importance of union of the states and thereby prompted what is known as confederation of the Canadian colonies. The Dominion of Canada came into being in 1867 with the consolidation of Ontario, Quebec, Nova Scotia, New Brunswick, and Manitoba. British Columbia joined four years later, and Prince Edward Island in 1873. In 1905, Alberta and Saskatchewan became members. Newfoundland finally joined in 1949. (Part of Labrador belongs to Quebec, part to Newfoundland.) The Northwest Ter-

ritories and the Yukon Territory are also part of the Dominion. At confederation, Canada was part of the British Empire. For it she sacrificed much in two world wars.

The word "Canada" was first noted in 1535 when used by the explorer Jacques Cartier. Indians in Quebec applied it to their tribal holding. The Biblical reference to dominion (Psalms 72:8) is apt: "He shall have dominion also from sea to sea."

As stated earlier, the French first dominated the fur trade. They got along well with the Indians, learning from them. There were many intermarriages, and from these and marriages between Indians and English trappers came the people known to Canadians as Métis. The French trappers became renowned canoeists called *voyageurs*. They made trails between navigable bodies of water and carried their canoes, provisions, and skins over such trails, called *portages*. These *voyageurs* were employed by both the Hudson's Bay Company and its rival, the Montreal-based North West Company, which merged with Hudson's in 1821. The latter supplied not only English capital and management but immigrants from the Orkney Islands, who also proved to be fine boatmen.

At the time of confederation, the now powerful Hudson's Bay Company still owned an enormous area of Canada, but in 1869 the government purchased Rupert's Land from it. (It was not until 1991 that the Hudson's Bay Company stopped dealing in furs. It remains one of Canada's largest retailers, with numerous department stores.)

The North West Mounted Rifles were founded in 1873 to bring law and order to the expanding frontier. Known today as the Mounties (officially, the world-famous Royal Canadian Mounted Police), they constitute Canada's federal police force. They are also the provincial and

criminal police in all the provinces except Ontario and Quebec. They are the only police in the Yukon and Northwest Territories.

Until confederation, immigrants to Canada were mainly of British or French origin, with Germans to a lesser extent. The latter settled near Halifax and in Kitchener (called Berlin until 1916, when it was changed to honor the British warrior, Lord Kitchener). These three nationalities composed the first Canadian mosaic.

In 1896 the discovery of gold around the Klondike River in the Yukon Territory brought adventurers from all over the world. This, however, did not have a significant influence on the overall immigration pattern.

As in the United States, there was a strong move to unite the Atlantic and Pacific oceans by rail. The last spike—an iron one, not gold—was driven in 1887. Many Chinese participated in this endeavor, as they did in railway construction in the United States.

Related to the development of Canadian railways is an interesting sideline. Sandford Fleming, who had emigrated from Scotland, was a civil engineer and scientist who contributed much to the system. He is remembered today for originating in 1884 an internationally accepted scheme for standard time. Three years later he was knighted, becoming Sir Sandford Fleming.

Canada and the United States needed Fleming's scheme because long east-west train routes passed through areas with local times that differed by several hours. Fleming's standard time was based on that of Greenwich, England. With the earth divided into 24 time zones, each corresponds to 60 minutes. Time is the same throughout each zone and differs from the basic Greenwich Time by a fixed number of hours.

The railway opened up the West, and many immigrants

came, mainly to farm. With most of the free land in the United States gone, western settlement in Canada was attractive. Also, by 1900 too much timber had been cut in the United States. Until well after World War II, lumber camps provided work for many immigrants to Canada.

We emphasize that immigration to Canada involved far fewer people than in the States. Between 1820 and 1970 a total of about five million newcomers reached Canada. In comparison, during the first decade of this century alone more than eight and a half million people entered the United States. Some of the difference reflects the fact that currently Canada's population is roughly twelve times less than that of the United States.

Early in this century Germans and Slavs entered Canada. Ukrainians settled in Ontario, Alberta, and Manitoba, while other Russians made their homes in Ontario, British Columbia, and Saskatchewan. The Dukhobors, a religious sect, flocked to the latter province. (Mennonites, Hutterites, and Mormons also found refuge in wide-open spaces.) Scandinavians and Dutch were attracted to rural parts of the prairie provinces and of British Columbia. Poles went to Ontario and the prairies. Jews and Italians preferred urban areas, especially in Ontario and Quebec.

British and American immigrants were long favored. One authority has pointed out that before 1940 it was government policy to promote conformity with English ideals as a way to assimilate foreigners. He also made it clear that racist immigration policies, anti-Oriental sentiment, and anti-Catholic and antiradical nativism have all long held sway in Canada.

For example, in 1902 Chinese and Japanese immigrants were declared unfit for full citizenship and dangerous to the state. Canada, like the United States, did little to

respond to the needs of Jews victimized by Hitler. In general, labor was opposed to immigration but did encourage aliens to work in agriculture rather than industry. The province of Quebec has traditionally been hostile to immigration.

Immigration, as in the United States, was largely dependent on "pull" factors—economic conditions in the new land—and on "push" factors—conditions at home.

Because of their emphasis on humanitarian values, the churches were active supporters of immigration.

In the 1960s restrictions were lifted as educational preference replaced racial discrimination as the chief criterion in the selection of immigrants. Ethnic diversity became a source of pride as the nation became multicultural. Toronto, whose inhabitants were once said to out-British the British, is now a truly cosmopolitan city.

Historically, relations with the Indians were better than in the United States. But, as in that country, the Native Americans of Canada did not fare well, many dying or becoming degraded as the result of the white man's conquest. For many years, the government took what could be considered a paternalistic attitude. More than seventy percent of Canadian Indians now live on reserves supervised by the Department of Indian Affairs and Northern Development.

The Inuit were virtually isolated until air travel to the Arctic became possible. These Eskimos, who were once wards of the state, now govern themselves and have three elected representatives on the territorial council.

What of the parent-child relationship among immigrant families? According to Kurelek and Engelhart's *They Sought a New World:*

"As the children became adults, most would learn to understand and appreciate their parents. The parents, in turn, would learn to respect the rights of their children to make certain decisions concerning their lives. But the learning on both sides could be painful."

Does that sound familiar?

CHAPTER ◇ 12

A Celebration of Culture

At home [my parents] spoke Spanish . . . The words would come quickly, with ease. Conveyed through those sounds was the pleasing, soothing, consoling reminder of being home.
—Richard Rodriguez, author of *Hunger of Memory*, 1982

According to government figures, during 1990–91, 12.6 percent of immigrants arriving in the United States came from the Dominican Republic (3.4 percent), Haiti (1.9 percent), West Indies (4.5 percent), and Africa (2.4 percent). The 1990 Census recorded 22.4 million Hispanics living in the United States. That is a large increase over the 1980 Census. California, New York, Texas, and Florida are home to many, but Hispanics are beginning to fan out to almost every region of the country. Some are migrant workers who move from place to place. Hispanics represent various classes and races. Nancy Foner, an anthropologist, notes that the social distinctions within populations are class, race, culture, age, and gender. These distinctions are especially evident among Hispanics.   111

They come from twenty-two countries: Puerto Rico, the Dominican Republic, Haiti, Jamaica, and Colombia, to name a few. Mexico, however, is the homeland of the great majority.

Mexico reflects an advanced Indian culture. For example, the Maya built huge stone pyramids and they invented a calendar. The Aztecs in 1325 founded what is now Mexico City. By 1521, Hernando Cortes and his Spanish conquistadors had destroyed the Aztec empire. Spanish rule continued for 300 years. Led by Fathers Miguel Hidalgo y Costilla and Morelos y Payon and finally by General Augustin Iturbide, the people formed a republic in 1823.

Mexico then included much of what is now the American Southwest. In 1846–48, a war between the United States and Mexico forced the latter to give up its land north of the Rio Grande. In 1917, after years of oppression, the people won a new constitution that provided a measure of social reform.

The land is rugged and rainfall is low, which makes agriculture difficult. In addition, crops and farm prices are controlled, as are imports and exports. It is hoped that when Mexico's vast oil reserves are developed, employment opportunities will improve. Meanwhile, countless people have left Mexico (and also regions of the Caribbean) for the United States to escape grinding and unrelenting poverty.

Once in the United States, Hispanics found discrimination and insults. For instance, Mexicans were often called by the derogatory term "wetback" in reference to the fact that some swam or waded in the Rio Grande to enter Texas illegally. Those who could not speak English were especially prone to exploitation by employers.

Many Hispanics soon realized their powerlessness. Fol-

lowing the example of Irish-Americans who had once been in the same plight, many Hispanics began to take a serious part in politics. Their aim was passage of legislation written especially for their benefit. Each year sees more Hispanics in office, and political candidates now actively seek the Hispanic vote.

Generalizations about the economic state of Hispanics are not possible. In Miami, for example, many former Cubans are highly successful. Yet in that same city, some recently arrived Mexicans live in dire poverty. Most Hispanic immigrants prosper; however, if they are not as successful as they had hoped to be, their children, for whom they sacrificed so much, usually are.

Family ties are very strong. The Roman Catholic Church claims the membership of most Hispanics and plays a prominent part in family life, although recently a considerable number of people have left the Chuch. Because of this, efforts have been made to recruit Hispanic priests, as well as English-speaking priests who also speak Spanish, and to have instruction given in Spanish rather than in English. For some Hispanics, Christo Rey, the great crucifix in the mountains of the border area between Mexico, Texas, and New Mexico, perhaps means more than the Statue of Liberty.

Mingled with family unity is a love of the Spanish language. Journalist John Weyr quotes one Hispanic immigrant's moving comments about his mother tongue: "[Spanish is] our own private language, the language in which my children speak about love, about growing up, about conveying their feelings as a family." Richard Rodriguez in his autobiography *Hunger of Memory*, makes the same point.

With this background, it is not surprising that most Hispanic immigrants resist conforming to the majority or dominant American culture. Although some speak in

Dr. Phill Carlos Archbold emigrated from Colon, Panama thirty years ago. An associate pastor for Hispanic and Special Ministries in the First Church of the Brethren, he is also the founder and CEO of The Positive Place, an AIDS Center in Brooklyn. He was chosen *Group Magazine's* "Youth Leader of the Year" in 1990, and has received numerous awards and citations for his community service and efforts.

dialects—variants of Spanish—and although more than 90 percent of American-born Hispanics are fluent in English, many Hispanics insist on using Spanish. Hispanics are also strong promoters of their own culture and values. If you are Hispanic, take pride that your people have been so successful in preserving you identity and heritage.

Hispanics occupy many important positions in government, industry, education, art, as well as many other areas. The Bush Administration paid tribute by appointing Antonia Novello, M.D., a pediatrician, to the position of Surgeon General of the United States Public Health Service, Dr. Novello was born Antonia Coello in Fajardo, Puerto Rico.

During the second half of this century, black Americans have shown increased interest in their African heritage. In the same way as piñatas, Mexican foods and dances, and other aspects of Mexican culture have become known to non-Hispanic Americans, so may African names become familiar. Many Afro-Americans have taken African names and begun to wear the national colors of Africa, green, black, and gold, to regain a sense of their heritage and their pride in it. In 1990 the *National Geographic* reported that an Afro-American mother in Philadelphia gave her children the African names of Atiba and Hessan, and had them wear dreadlocks as a way of exposing them to African traditions. Atiba means "one of understanding"; Hessan means "brave, generous, and kind".

Mark Mathabane, an author from South Africa, gives insight about the feelings of a black immigrant of our times in his autobiographical book, *Kaffir Boy in America*. Books such as this and *Hunger of Memory* should lead to better understanding in a multicultural society.

Mathabane lived in Alexandra, South Africa, in poverty and without much hope of a better life until he was eighteen.

Mark Mathebane, his wife Gail, authors of *Love in Black and White: The Triumph of Love over Prejudice and Taboo*, and their children, Nathan and Bianca.

At that time, a tennis scholarship provided him welcome escape from the oppressive burden of apartheid, or segregation. By determination and hard work, he obtained a college education, graduating from Dowling College in New York. A gifted and successful writer, Mathabane now lives in North Carolina with his wife and children. In *Love in Black and White*, published in 1992, Mark and Gail Mathabane discuss their interracial marriage.

This chapter began with a quotation from *Hunger of Memory*; we end it with one from *Kaffir Boy in America*. Mathabane notes that in spite of hardships and disappointments, his dream of coming to America and succeeding did in many ways materialize; "I'm happily married, I own a lovely house, I'm supporting my family and putting my siblings [brother and sisters] through school, I can write and talk freely, and my human and civil rights are protected under American law."

CHAPTER 13

Women Immigrants—In Double Jeopardy

She hath done what she could. . . .

—Mark 14:8

Progress in the advancement of women varies from country to country. Many women emigrate from cultures that see the role of a woman in a different light from what is now accepted in both the United States and Canada. Because of this, immigrant women may face double jeopardy, or hazards. As newcomers they belong to a minority group, and as women they belong to a class, though not numerically small, that is generally regarded as lacking in power. In this chapter we shall take a brief look at the changing status of American women and then see what it is today.

117

Jamestown in Virginia was the oldest English settlement in the New World. Its people had suffered great hardships, and for a time it appeared that the colony might perish. Fortunately conditions began to improve, and in 1620 the founding London Company sent out ninety young women to marry colonists who were unknown to these would-be wives. Guaranteed to be "pure and spotless," each cost her spouse 120 pounds of tobacco.

The transaction shows the desirability of the presence of women in a community. On the other hand, a bride would have had little recourse had she found conditions different from her expectations. Similar arranged marriages have occurred in America in the past and still take place occasionally. They have often been successful, but the practice is degrading to womanhood.

Plymouth, Massachusetts, was the site of another English settlement. Today in Plymouth stands a statue dedicated to the Pilgrim mothers who reared their children according to the beliefs of the Protestant faith. This underscores what the Pilgrims perceived to be the role of a woman—that of mother. With a very high infant mortality rate, many pregnancies were necessary to produce the children who would in time carry on. So it is likely that the Pilgrim mothers were pregnant much of the time of their harsh existence.

For many years in the history of Canada and the United States, survival for women (and men too) required hard, unrelenting work. As long as there was a frontier in the American continent, women were involved in westward expansion. In addition to bearing and raising their children, women farmed and performed many tasks related to the actual survival of the family. The value of this type of contribution was at least recognized by men.

(It is a matter of interest that the first state to grant women the vote was Wyoming, a frontier state whose pioneer women had done a great deal.)

But a wife had few rights. For example, if she inherited money—or even earned it—common law decreed that it belonged to her husband. It was well into the nineteenth century before there were legal changes in this. In an atmosphere where the literal meaning of the Bible was accepted, women were at a disadvantage. They were forced to listen to Genesis 3:16: ". . . in sorrow thou shalt bring forth children; and thy desire shall be to thy husband, and he shall rule over thee." And they were governed by pronouncements from St. Paul such as: "Wives, submit yourselves unto your own husbands. . . . For the husband is head of the wife. . . ." (Ephesians 5:22,23), and, "But I suffer not a woman to teach, nor to usurp authority over the man, but to be in silence." (I Timothy 2:12).

No matter how harsh their existence, few women resorted to divorce because of the disgrace associated with it. It was legal in some states, but only on grounds of bigamy, adultery, impotence, desertion, or extreme cruelty. Alcoholism, for instance, was not necessarily a valid reason. In the event that divorce was granted, custody of the children was given to the father.

As for the woman who remained single—known as a spinster—there was little opportunity in the 1800s for her to be independent as she can be today. During the first half of that century there were some opportunities for teachers of young children, seamstresses, and house-keepers. Later, some factory work was available, and the nursing profession was beginning to grow. Since higher education for women was limited, entrance to most professions was denied. So unmarried women generally

received poor wages and often were forced to live with their families where the word of a father or brother was law.

Married women seldom worked outside the home. That was considered degrading and an insult to the husband, whose duty it was to provide for his family. The essential point here, however, is that a wife in an agricultural society could not be spared to pursue outside work. She was very much needed to keep a family together in a day when clothing was produced at home, when food preparation was sometimes done over open fires or at best was dependent on cumbersome wood-burning stoves, when refrigerators did not exist. When a wife died—and many did die in their prime—she was usually replaced very quickly; a widower with a large number of children found it almost impossible to manage without a spouse. Today one does not have to look far to find gravestones of men with as many as three wives buried around them.

As the United States and Canada became more industrialized, more and more men lived in cities and towns where they earned their living in various businesses. At the same time, housekeeping became somewhat easier for their wives. This situation gave the false impression that the wife's labor amounted to little; she was at home all day, not away earning money as her husband did.

Many nineteenth-century women were dissatisfied with their lot. Two hundred fifty of them met in Seneca Falls, New York, in 1848 to hold the first convention on women's rights. It would be seventy-two years before the Constitution was amended to allow women to vote, but it was a beginning. The leaders of the movement were Susan B. Anthony, who was not married, and Elizabeth Cady Stanton, who was married, and who would also

devote much of her energy to reform of the divorce laws.

There had been great expectation that winning the right to vote would do much to emancipate women. Important as it was, however, it did little to elevate their status. It did, of course, make possible the election of female public officials, and that is becoming increasingly important today.

Two factors did contribute more significantly to woman's liberation. The first was gaining the right to the same opportunities in education as were open to males. The second was the accessibility of birth control. Although various methods of contraception had been available for years, it was not until the advent of "the pill" in the 1960s that large numbers of women controlled the size of their families.

Major wars have speeded up the liberation of women. During the Civil War women abolitionists banded together to support the cause of the North. They learned about organization and fundraising, at the same time gaining confidence in themselves. When that terrible war was over, they directed their newfound skills to working for women's rights.

In both World Wars that followed, women made outstanding contributions to the war effort. Some served with the armed forces, and many worked in all sorts of essential industries. Following World War I, the women of the United States obtained the vote. (On the other hand, the province of Quebec did not grant women the right to vote until 1940. For interesting viewpoints on the progress of feminism in Canada, read *Mother Was Not a Person*, compiled by Margaret Andersen.) Service during World War II reinforced women's confidence in themselves and gained the respect of their countrymen. Many women who had for the first time earned good

wages (in war industries) became discontented at the idea of spending the rest of their lives at home.

By the 1960s middle-class housewives who had worked outside their homes for only limited periods were beginning to be bored with their lives. Vacuum cleaners and automatic washers, manufactured clothing and so forth had made their lives much easier than the lives of their mothers and grandmothers. No longer were they content to live through their husbands and children; they wanted meaningful careers that would bring them self-fulfillment.

An influential book by Betty Friedan, *The Feminine Mystique*, explained their position and provided a framework for action. Mrs. Friedan became a leader of the feminist movement (also called women's liberation movement), and she founded NOW, the National Organization for Women.

Women's liberation demands full equality with men. It seeks to move women with feminist beliefs into policy-making positions in government, education, religion, and all other powerful institutions of society. It fights for economic rights such as equality in jobs, insurance, Social Security, and the like. In sports it seeks equal opportunities for girls; it also pursues ways to present feminist role models to schoolchildren. It has directed much energy to preventing rape and spouse abuse and to fighting sexual harassment and female exploitation. It has been an advocate of access to safe and legal abortion, maternity leave, day care for children, and flexible work schedules. It has also been active in fighting discrimination against homosexuals.

Much progress has been made. Women have graduated from the service academies; there are women astronauts; a woman has been Surgeon General of the United States; there are female state governors, United States Senators,

---

PROPOSED EQUAL RIGHTS AMENDMENT OF 1972

1. Equality of rights under the law shall not be denied or abridged by the United States or any State on account of sex.
2. The Congress shall have the power to enforce, by appropriate legislation, the provisions of this article.
3. The amendment shall take effect two years after the date of ratification.

For this to have become law, ratification, or formal approval, by thirty-eight states was necessary. Even after Congress granted extension of the deadline, the amendment died in 1982 because of insufficient support from the states. Femininsts believe that an Equal Rights Amendment (ERA) would prevent such inequalities as denying women in the armed services the right to fight in combat.

---

and all manner of elected officials; women sit in board rooms and occupy top positions in management; they serve in law enforcement and are successful in many professions—law, medicine, engineering, and so on. In short, they have done what they could. So far, however, only a handful of women have attained positions of power, a fact that spurs feminists to greater efforts.

Today nearly all married women find that they must work—most for economic reasons, some because they cannot find satisfaction in being only wife and mother and seek meaningful work beyond their families.

Serious problems are involved in women's liberation. As more and more women become heads of households, the standard of living for most of them declines. The

reasons vary; it may be because of a teenage pregnancy, because of divorce, whatever. The tragedy is that these women and their children suffer, some to the extent that they lack even basic medical care. Also, in most families today, including those with two parents, there is no longer a parent at home during the day. All too often the result is inadequate supervision of children. Solving the problem of providing proper care for coming generations is one of the great challenges of the day.

The ideas represented by the women's movement may be completely familiar to you, especially if you are female. But they may be completely foreign to your mother and father. If so, your mother may accept these ideas more readily than your father. The chances are great that they will cause conflict between you and your parents—one more roadblock an immigrant has to face. It is just possible that you can win over your mother with patient explanations. Then it is time for her and you to work on your father. Good luck!

CHAPTER 14

The United States Today—Land of the Noble Free*

The land flourished because it was fed from so many sources . . . so many cultures and traditions and peoples.
—President Lyndon B. Johnson, 1965

Today's population mix is largely a result of past immigration policy. As will be clear, Congress frequently changes the laws. Here are some of the major pieces of legislation that have been enacted. Not included are special acts such as those that governed war brides and various groups of displaced persons.

---

*From "My Country! 'Tis of Thee" by Samuel Francis Smith (1808–1895.)

Immigration Act of 1875. This first national restriction of immigration barred criminals and prostitutes. It entrusted inspection of immigrants to collectors of the ports.

Immigration Act of 1882. Barred "lunatics and idiots" and others likely to become "public charges."

Chinese Exclusion Act of 1882. Prevented entry of Chinese laborers. (Repealed in 1943.)

Immigration Acts of 1885 and 1887. Labor laws that made it unlawful to admit aliens under contract. The intent was to prevent employers from importing large numbers of low-paid immigrants who would depress the American labor market.

Immigration Act of 1891. The first law to bar persons with certain diseases; also felons, paupers, polygamists, and those guilty of "moral turpitude." It authorized the deportation of illegal aliens.

Immigration Act of 1903. Barred persons with certain mental diseases, epilepsy, etc.; also anarchists and "white slave traders."

Immigration Act of 1907. Barred persons with tuberculosis, unaccompanied children under sixteen, and persons considered not capable of earning a living.

Immigration Act of 1917. Codified previous exclusion provisions; established literacy as a basis for entry.

Immigration Act of 1921. The first quota law, it limited annual immigration to three percent of national origin of foreign born present in U.S. in 1910.

Immigration Act of 1924. Assigned quotas to each nationality in proportion to its contribution to

the existing U.S. population, based on the 1920 Census. Aliens ineligible for citizenship were barred. Unlimited entry of Canadians and Latin Americans was permitted.

Immigration and Neutrality Act of 1952. Codified all existing legislation; eliminated race as a bar to immigration.

Immigration and Nationality Act Amendments of 1965. Abolished national origin as the basis for quotas. On a first come, first served basis, annual numerical ceilings were set:

> 120,000 for natives of the Western Hemisphere
> 170,000 for natives of the Eastern Hemisphere
> with a per-country limit of 20,000

New preference categories were established:

> Relatives of immigrants, 74 percent
> Scientists, artists, 10 percent
> Skilled and unskilled labor, 10 percent
> Refugees, 6 percent

(This legislation was responsible for what is sometimes called "new" immigration, to distinguish it from the immigration of so many Europeans that had preceded.)

Presidential Directive of 1979. Admitted thousands of Vietnamese "boat people."

Refugee Act of 1980. Set up a systematic procedure for the admission of refugees seeking asylum from persecution at home. It allocated 50,000 visas

Filipinos waiting at the U.S. Consulate in Manila to apply for immigration visas. Nursing in the United States has benefited immensely from the immigration of Filipinos (courtesy Library of Congress).

for "normal-flow" refugees and empowered the President, after consultation with Congress, to increase the annual allocation. It reduced the worldwide ceiling to 270,000 immigrants annually.

Immigration Reform and Control Act of 1986. Prohibited the hiring of illegal immigrants and offered amnesty to illegal immigrants who had lived in the United States continuously since January 1, 1982.

Immigration Reform and Control Act of 1990. Set a first-ever entry "cap" of 700,000 immigrants for the next three years and 675,000 yearly thereafter. The cap can be "pierced" to benefit family unification. Immigrants legalized under the 1986 Act will receive an additional twelve months to become permanent residents, and their spouses and children may stay in the U.S. until permanent visas are available. Employment-related slots were increased to 140,000 per year. First preference is to be given to immigrants with "extraordinary ability," then to those with advanced degrees, then to those with a baccalaureate degree, and last to a small number of unskilled workers. There are 10,000 new openings for "special immigrants" and 10,000 for foreigners willing to invest in a new U.S. business that will provide at least ten new jobs.

The 1965 law no longer gave preference to Northern and Central Europeans, but encouraged Latin Americans and Asians to immigrate in far greater numbers. In the last ten years the number of Hispanic immigrants increased by 53 percent, and the number of immigrant

Asians and Pacific Islanders by almost 108 percent. The effect is reflected in the figure for the white percentage of the population: It has fallen from 83 percent in 1980 to about 80 percent in 1990. It is predicted that by the beginning of the 21st century a greater decrease will have occurred. Nevertheless, it seems unlikely that the majority—white and English-speaking—culture will be undermined in the near future.

The Immigration and Naturalization Service (INS) is under the Department of Justice. The INS enforces the laws that govern immigration and naturalization.

Since 1902 a period of five years of residency in the United States is required before an immigrant can become an American citizen. He or she must also demonstrate the ability to read and write English. Children under eighteen become citizens automatically on the naturalization of the head of the family.

Immigrants to Canada are divided into three groups: family members who are dependents, independents, and refugees. Skilled workers are favored. Investors with proven business acumen who are willing to lend $250,000 or more to Canadian industry for a period of five years receive visas. Hong Kong residents are particularly sought for the Immigrant Investor Program, which promises permanent citizenship after three years. No negative consideration is given to the country or hemisphere of the émigré.

For 1991, Canada planned to admit 250,000 aliens, increased from a maximum of 175,000. Of the 26 million population of Canada in 1990, 40 percent had origin in the British Isles, 27 percent were of French descent, and

---

Oath of Allegiance to the United States

This oath is administered by a judge when an immigrant becomes a citizen.

I hereby declare, on oath, that I absolutely and entirely renounce and abjure all allegiance and fidelity to any foreign prince, potentate, state or sovereignty to whom or which I have heretofore been a subject or citizen; that I will support and defend the Constitution and laws of the United States of America against all enemies, foreign and domestic; that I will bear true faith and allegiance to the same; that I will bear arms on behalf of the United States when required by the law; that I will perform noncombatant service in the armed forces of the United States when required by the law; that I will perform work of national importance under civilian direction when required by the law, and that I take this obligation freely without any mental reservation or purpose of evasion; so help me God.

---

20 percent had roots in continental Europe. Less than 1 percent of the population was Indian and Inuit.

From generations that came before you, Canada sought immigrant farmers and the United States wanted immigrant laborers. With the advent of the technological age, both countries are looking for immigrants with sophisticated technical skills and also people with business experience and money to invest. It is no longer a question of America's asking other nations for their tired and their poor.

Author George Gilder, in *Microcosm: The Quantum Revolution in Economics and Technology*, writes that high-tech centers in the United States have utilized

the genius of inventive Hungarians, Chinese, Israelis, Italians, Greeks, and so on.

There has always been a danger that some countries may export their best intellects to the United States. At one time Canada was hard hit by this phenomenon, known as the brain drain. Today it is common for students from all over the world to be sent to the United States for advanced education often not offered in their native lands. It is also common for such students to stay permanently if official permission is obtained. This, of course, denies the immigrant's country the benefit of his or her ability and training. The People's Republic of China makes special efforts to have its students return after study abroad.

Current isues of magazines and newspapers are filled with success stories involving immigrants. Authorities note that the newly arrived are more than twice as likely to start businesses as are native-born Americans.

The motto of the United States—"*E pluribus Unum*"— means "Out of many, one." In recent years there has been a movement toward creating a multiethnic society, which is the antithesis of the motto. In such an environment each ethnic group would "do its own thing," with little effort to become Americanized. Generally speaking, advocates of multiethnicity do not stress the importance of learning English as fast as possible.

According to historian Arthur Schlesinger, Jr., the adoption of multiethnicity has good and bad sides. He writes, "The American culture at last began to give shamefully overdue recognition to the achievements of groups subordinated and spurned during the high noon of Anglo dominance, and it began to acknowledge the great swirling world beyond Europe." That he considers a plus. But he believes that multiethnicity may be carried

too far, declaring, "Group separation crystalizes the differences, magnifies tensions, intensifies hostilities."

United States Senator Alan K. Simpson of Wyoming once put it this way: "If immigration is continued at a high level and yet a substantial portion of the newcomers and their descendants do not assimilate, they may create in America some of the same social, political, and economic problems which existed in the country which they have chosen to depart."

Whether or not the United States will remain as it is now—one culture contributed to by many—or become a collection of many diverse cultures remains to be seen.

Canada, already a bilingual country, in recent years has become increasingly multiethnic. To illustrate, the immigrants who became citizens in 1988 represented 170 countries. The dominant background remains British, with French second. But the Canadian mosaic is being enriched with non-British and non-French Europeans, with Africans, Asians, and West Indians. Pride in ethnic origin is reinforced and encouraged to a greater extent than in the United States.

Suppose you had arrived from Greece in the early part of this century. Suppose also that you knew only a few words of English. You would have been sent to school and subjected to the regular curriculum with all classes in English and no special help because you were a foreigner. No doubt you would have found this "sink-or-swim" (or "total immersion") method traumatic, but it is the way countless immigrant children learned English. (There is little mention of how many dropped out because of the harshness of the system.)

Mexican-American activists came to believe that instruction in English only contributed to the high dropout rates they were seeing among Spanish-speaking students.

By 1968 these activists had exerted enough pressure on Congress to achieve passage of the Bilingual Education Act.

The Act provided funds for programs designed to teach Hispanic schoolchildren in Spanish. (The congressional mandate was to "transition" Hispanic children into English.) These pupils learn social studies, science, and math in their native language, a process that may take four to seven years before a child can reach national averages on standardized tests given in English.

A 1974 Supreme Court decision made it mandatory for the public schools to provide special help for immigrant children. At present about 73 percent of language-minority children are Hispanic. In cities with heavy concentrations of Hispanics only, bilingual teaching should work well.

Of the world's some 200 languages, about 150 are spoken within the borders of the United States. (The Hmong had no alphabet or written language until 1959.) In most schools it is prohibitively expensive to hire bilingual teachers for fewer than twenty students who speak the same language in the same grade. In seven states, 25 percent or more of students are of language minorities, and during the 1990s about 3.5 million children from homes where English is not the first language are expected to enter the public schools. So you can readily see the complexity of the problem of instructing foreign children.

How can the schools deal with this? Educators seem to agree that a young immigrant child may be able to make himself or herself understood in English in as short a time as a few months. Beyond the fourth grade, however, learning English becomes more difficult.

English as a Second Language (ESL) is widely used. In

FROM THE PEN OF WILLIAM SHAKESPEARE

The quality of mercy is not strain'd,
It droppeth as the gentle dew from heaven
Upon the place beneath. It is twice bless'd:
It blesseth him that gives and him that takes.
'Tis mightiest in the mightiest: it becomes
The throned monarch better than his crown;
His sceptre shows the force of temporal power,
The attribute to awe and majesty,
Wherein doth sit the dread and fear of kings;
But mercy is above this sceptred sway,
It is enthroned in the hearts of kings,
It is an attribute to God himself;
And earthly power doth then show likest God's,
When mercy seasons justice. . . .

From *The Merchant of Venice*

This above all: to thine own self be true,
And it must follow, as the night the day,
Thou canst not then be false to any man.

From *Hamlet*

Blow, blow, thou winter wind!
Thou art not so unkind
As man's ingratitude.

From *As You Like It*

---

this program all instruction is in English, but the teacher has special training that enables the child to understand something of what is being said. All immigrant children, regardless of their native tongue, may be mixed in an ESL class given at a specific grade level. In some New York schools with immigrants from diverse countries, this

LINCOLN'S ADDRESS AT GETTYSBURG, 1863

Fourscore and seven years ago our fathers brought forth on this continent a new nation, conceived in liberty and dedicated to the proposition that all men are created equal.

Now we are engaged in a great civil war, testing whether that nation or any nation so conceived and so dedicated can long endure. We are met on a great battlefield of that war. We have come to dedicate a portion of that field as a final restingplace for those who here gave their lives that that nation might live. It is altogether fitting and proper that we should do this.

But, in a larger sense, we cannot dedicate—we cannot consecrate—we cannot hallow—this ground. The brave men, living and dead, who struggled here, have consecrated it, far above our poor power to add or detract. The world will little note, nor long remember, what we say here, but it can never forget what they did here. It is for us the living, rather, to be dedicated here to the unfinished work which they who fought here have thus far so nobly advanced. It is rather for us to be here dedicated to the great task remaining before us—that from these honored dead we take increased devotion to that cause for which they gave the last full measure of devotion—that we here highly resolve that these dead shall not have died in vain—that this nation, under God, shall have a new birth of freedom—and that government of the people, by the people, for the people shall not perish from the earth.

might be a good solution. A child may need to spend three or four years in an ESL class.

Some schools have found that parents can be a great help as translators. Have you a relative whose language ability could assist the school system in some way?

FROM THE PEN OF WINSTON CHURCHILL

From Stettin on the Baltic to Trieste on the Adriatic an iron curtain has descended across the Continent. Behind that line lie all the capitals of the ancient states of Central and Western Europe....

March 5, 1946, Fulton, Missouri

...and the Canadian Pacific Railway was opened in 1885. Other lines sprang up, and corn, soon counted in millions of bushels a year, begam to flow in from the prairies. Canada had become a nation, and shining prospects lay before her.

A History of the English-Speaking Peoples, 1956–58

The Americans took but little when they emigrated from Europe except what they stood up in and what they had in their souls. They came through, they tamed the wilderness, they became "a refuge for the oppressed from every land and clime." They have become today the greatest State and power in the world, speaking our language, cherishing our common law, and possessing, like our great Dominions, in broad principle, the same ideals.

House of Commons, October 28, 1947

But the only thing I would whip [boys] for is not knowing English. I would whip them hard for that.

My Early Life, 1930

Obviously, imaginative ideas are needed—ideas that can be adapted to the situation at hand.

At least one of every seven persons on this planet today uses English. Of the world's languages, English has the largest vocabulary. It is accepted as the universal language of business and commerce. Half of the books

produced are written in English, and since the invention of the printing press a rich literature has demonstrated the majesty of the language.

The whole world has long admired the plays and poetry of William Shakespeare (1564–1616). A few excerpts from his works are presented here. Two centuries later, Abraham Lincoln used the English language to produce prose that gained the respect of great scholars. During this century, Winston Churchill's writings won him a Nobel Prize in literature. Excerpts from the works of the latter two are also given here. For examples of sublime expression written in English, read some of Churchill's wartime speeches and Lincoln's Second Inaugural Address.

With an excellent track record in commerce, science, and literature, English is likely to remain for your lifetime, anyway, the dominant language in both the United States and Canada. A 1976 study conducted by the Census Bureau demonstrated a strong connection between low proficiency in English and low earnings. So mastery of English is definitely a major factor in your economic success. And seeking to improve your English should in no way interfere with your progress in obtaining a firm foundation in the language of your parents.

In the past attempts have been made to construct a universal or international language suitable for use as a second language. So far these artificial languages have not gained great popularity. Of them, Esperanto is probably the most used. It is relatively easy to learn, is particularly favored in Central Europe and Japan, and is used in travel and correspondence.

The originator was a Jewish physician, Ludwik Zamenhof (1859–1915). His pseudonym was Dr.

Esperanto, which means "one who hopes." After witnessing great ethnic conflict in his Polish birthplace, Bialystok in the province of Grodans, he had hoped to promote tolerance and understanding among nations by developing Esperanto, which he did at age nineteen. According to Zamenhof, he was convinced early in his life that:

> ". . . the diversity of languages is . . . the main cause that separates the human family and divides it into conflicting groups . . . I was taught that all men were brothers, and meanwhile, in the street, in the square, everything at every step made me feel that men did not exist, only Russians, Poles, Germans, Jews and so on . . . I kept telling myself that when I was grown up I would certainly destroy this evil."

You may obtain information on Esperanto from:

Esperanto League for North America
P.O. Box 1129-M
El Cerrito, CA 94530

Canadian Esperanto Association
P.O. Box 2159-A
Sidney, BC V8L 3S3

Perhaps in time the world will be forced to use an international language if still greater confusion arises with the use of multiple language in one area. At present, however, English comes closest to being an international language.

KING JAMES VERSION OF THE BIBLE

Our Father which art in heaven, Hallowed be thy name. Thy kingdom come. Thy will be done in earth, as it is in heaven. Give us this day our daily bread. And forgive us our debts, as we forgive our debtors. And lead us not into temptation, but deliver us from evil: For thine is the kingdom, and the power, and the glory, for ever. Amen.

ESPERANTO

Patro nia, kiu estas en la ĉielo, sankta estu via nomo; venu reĝeco via; estu volo via, kiel en la ĉielo, tiel ankaŭ sur la tero. Panon nian ĉiutagan donu al ni hodiaŭ; kaj pardonu al ni ŝuldojn niajn, kiel ni ankaŭ pardonas al niaj ŝuldantoj; kaj ne konduku nin en la tenton, sed liberigu nin de la malbono. Ĉar via estas la regeco, la povo kaj la gloro eterne. Amen!

The print and electronic media make us aware of how many immigrants have recently made and are making their mark on American life. Here is a sampling given in no special order:

Isamu Noguchi	Sculpture	Japan
Alistair Cooke	Journalism	Great Britain
Nyung Whum Chang	Music	Korea
Zubin Mehta	Music	India
Arnold Schwarzenegger	Acting and Body Building	Austria

From *Encyclopaedia Britannica*, 15th ed. Macropaedia, vol. 9, p. 743.

Published in 1993 by The Rosen Publishing Group, Inc.
29 East 21st Street, New York, NY 10010

First Edition

Library of Congress Cataloging-in-Publication Data

Reynolds, Moira Davison.
    Coping with an immigrant parent / Moira Davison Reynolds.
        p.   cm.
    Includes bibliographical references and index.
        Summary: Explores the cultural conflicts that can occur within
    families when children of immigrants have to cope with parents
    having different morals and values.
        ISBN 0-8239-1462-3
        1. Children of immigrants—United States—Juvenile literature.
    2. Children of immigrants—United States—Family relationships—
    Juvenile literature. 3. Assimilation (Sociology) —Juvenile literature.
    4. Culture conflict—Juvenile literature. 5. United States—
    Emigration and immigration. —Juvenile literature. [1. United
    States—Emigration and immigration. 2. Parent and child. 3. Culture
    conflict.] I. Title
    HQ796.R535   1992
    306.874—dc20
                                                            92-4389
                                                            CIP
                                                            AC

Manufactured in the United States of America